What I Wasn't Expecting When I was Expecting:

A Grieving Widow's Memoir

Kristina Smith

D0721185

Dedication

This book is dedicated to my best friend, my husband, the greatest fighter I have ever known. To the man who loved me unconditionally and gave me the greatest gift of love. This is to you, handsome: We won. We always do.

To My Colon Brothers and Sisters, who helped me heal—more than I thought possible; we are forever family:

Diana

Stephen

Candice

Jessica

Ashley

Andy

Stacy

Michelle

Matthew

Wint

Riley

Our Angel Sister, Allison

Acknowledgements

There are so many people whom I have to thank in the process of making this book, my journey of healing, a reality. First, my editor, Amy Wescott. Amy, you have epitomized grace, love, and wisdom as if you have known me my entire life. You are magical at craft, revision, editing, but most importantly turning my hurt into beauty. I am forever indebted to you and the love you have handled our story with. I thank God for His perfect timing of our lives intersecting.

Dr. Ralph LeBlanc—my book publishing mentor! There are few people as selfless, creative, innovative and determined as you are to help make my dream a reality. The book covers, the planning, preparation, the outside-the-box thinking, as you highlight my desire to see healing in others, the book promotions—you are the muscles behind all of this! I cannot explain another like you, other than God, again, sending the exact right people into my life, at the exact right time.

Ali & Company Photography, thank you for capturing my smile that continues to lead me through my days. The talent you have with a camera in your hands, is astounding. I remember the days I wished to see me smile again—and you captured this moment. Thank you!

Porter, my forever love, I owe you my greatest thanks. Thank you for giving me grace, being patient, always rolling with the flow, wiping my tears, making me strong, and teaching me a sacrificial, unconditional love that only you could. Thank you for your tender heart, allowing me to be weak, reminding me to be strong, to always live, laugh and make memories, but above all for always carrying your Daddy with us, as we tackle each day. You are, and will always be, my lifeline. You are my miracle and encompass every beat of my heart. I love you, sweet boy.

And most importantly, God. God, thank you a million times over will still fall short of what I owe you in thankfulness. I have cried, begged, cursed, questioned, and even thanked all that You have created for my life. Thank you for the strength, when strength wasn't there to even take another step. Thank you for grace. Thank you, God, for grace! You have given me more grace than everyone on Earth deserves. I couldn't live this life without that gift you give to me daily. Thank you, God, for love, memories, a husband, a child, a family, I could only dream of. Thank you for your perfect timing, of events and of the amazing people you have put into my life to walk this journey of life with me. Thank you, above all, for your promises and forgiveness through Salvation. This work is for you, and our hopes of everyone joining you in Eternity.

Preface

In the past few years, after suffering the loss of my husband Joe to colon cancer, many have told me that I have a story to tell. I have been told the love between my husband and me is something most people only dream of, something that many never experience. Our love story is often called a fairytale. Maybe it is, but our love story is my hard reality.

Despite our story of pain, suffering, personal sacrifice, hopelessness, helplessness, and anger that we have been robbed of our life together, our love story prevails. It's my favorite story of all. And through it all, I've experienced the mercy of our Heavenly Father, who has given me the faith, hope, and love I needed every step of the way.

This book is written in honor of the greatest fight of love I've ever witnessed or experienced. I wrote this book primarily for my own healing, but I hope many others will experience healing after reading the words I was able to pour out onto these pages. I've always expected nothing but greatness for my life—our life—and greatness is exactly what I have.

May my words bring comfort, empathy, sympathy, healing, hope, strength, or whatever it is that will help heal your broken heart. I also pray that my words will give you a greater capacity to help others—both friends and strangers—as they walk through their own pain and suffering. May our story spur each of us on to love others well.

Table of Contents

Chapter 1

June 22, 2013

The date—June 22, 2013—will forever ring in my head. We are up all night. Joe runs from hospital bed to toilet, back and forth, back and forth. I anxiously sit, wide awake, and watch the hands of the clock tick, helpless. Joe lies in the bed between sprints to the restroom, failing to convince me he has ever fallen asleep. Another night of silence between us; we don't know what to think nor what to say.

After the long night of colonoscopy-prep, the nurses come to our room at 9:00 a.m. to take Joe for the procedure. Joe's parents arrive. My nagging morning sickness rises to its peak. My pregnant body is exhausted. My heart is racing fast with dread, overwhelming me. I somehow know we are not going to receive good news today. I am terrified. My body begins to shake. I will my mind and body to take hold, to gain composure. *My husband needs me.*

I quickly kiss Joe good-bye, as if my swiftness will prevent the tears from coming. Walking down the hallway, the doctor meets me and assures me, "It shouldn't take long. I will be right out to get you once we are done."

Nodding my head, I wearily walk out to my waiting spot along a white vacant hallway and fall onto a couch. My fear takes over. I pull my knees as close to my chest as my swollen body will allow and sob. Joe's parents sit next to me, attempting to comfort each other in a moment where no comfort is found.

Tears done, emotions still high, I get up. I pace.

I fidget with my cell phone.

I need to pee.

I can't. *What if they come to get me? What if he needs me?*

I sit back down.

Joe's dad tries to soothe me by putting his hand on my leg, then around my shoulders. His mom goes to the bathroom. I try to swallow the lump that is lodged in my throat.

The door opens. The doctor quietly requests, "Mrs. Smith, can you come on back with me, please?"

My father-in-law and I stand and follow the doctor. I pass my groggy Joe on a long, white hospital bed in the hallway. I brush my hand over his face, his cheek. I kiss his forehead. He barely opens his eyes, smiles, and goes back to sleep.

"Next doorway on your right," I hear a small voice direct from behind me.

Turning right, Joe's dad and I sit in the only two chairs available in the tiny one-person office. A small fan ruffles stacks of papers' edges with every rotation, while the nurses' voices drift in from across the hallway. The sterile hospital smell sickens my stomach more, and I tense my shoulders and hold my breath, bracing myself for what the doctor is about to divulge.

Leaning against the white wall in front of us, the doctor clears his throat, "So, we were able to do the colonoscopy with no complications. We did find a tumor on your husband's colon."

I continue to nod and blink, my mind racing. *Okay, that's fine. That's it?*

As if answering the question in my head, he announces, "And the tumor is cancerous."

Immediately, I scream, "No!" and fall forward toward the floor. Joe's dad catches me, holding my body before it topples out of my chair. My head is on his left knee. "NO. NO! NO! You do not understand! We are seven months pregnant! We are having a baby!" keeps spilling out of my mouth.

Joe's dad speaks through his own cracking voice, "That's okay. It's just that, that word is pretty scary."

Quietly, the doctor leaves us with, "I will send a doctor up to the room later to discuss options with you. At this time, we will wheel Joe back up to the room. Just meet him up there."

I pass Joe again right outside that cramped office. Trying to open his eyes from the anesthesia, he doesn't notice me as I quickly wobble past him. I try not to cry as I pass, as if hiding the tears would somehow make it untrue, or at least prevent him from learning this terrible news. I seal my lips to try to stifle the screaming cries that are pushing up through my throat. Joe's dad and I walk back through the double metal doors.

Waiting alone in the hallway, I can be silent no longer. I run past Joe's mom towards the exterior doors, sobs racking my body enough that I begin dry heaving. I need fresh air, but the doors are locked. My head spinning, I collapse to the floor and scream. I scream and cry until Joe's dad, who is dealing with his own broken heart, comes to comfort me in the middle of that lonely, isolated hallway. Upon standing, I see Joe's mom leaning against the wall, sobbing because her little boy has cancer. I look around at our little army of three, and in a moment of sudden clarity, I command, "We need to get back up to Joe's room before he gets there."

Stifling the tears, but anticipating the pain of what is next, I walk into our hospital room where Joe is being rolled in on his hospital bed right behind me. Joe's dad whispers, "We'll let you guys have a few minutes. We will step out." There I am, staring at my husband with a stranger-like awkwardness between us. There are no doctors, nurses, or medical staff to deliver the news—just me and the man I married 349 days prior. I sit on the right edge of the bed, facing him. We continue to stare back at each other, except when I look down and mess with the sheets.

How am I—his wife, his best friend, the mother of his unborn son, his soulmate—supposed to look him in the eyes and tell him he has cancer? I don't know. I still do not know.

Stalling, I fidget with his left hand and each of his calloused fingers, unable to swallow the lump in my throat or to fight the tears threatening to pour onto my cheeks. "Well, what'd they say?" Joe finally questions, breaking the silence.

I stare. I stare hard into those baby blues that I have lost myself in so many times before. I try to talk, but I physically cannot.

"Babe. What did they say?" he repeated.
I look down. *How do I do this? How do I tell him?* I look back up to his face, biting my quivering lip. I try to swallow the lump, again. I somehow manage, "It's umm. It's cancer." As I speak, I catch his eye and then lunge forward to put my arms around his neck.

He shakes his head, "No. NO! What? NO!" My head is on his left shoulder. My tears are uncontrollable. Nodding my head yes, he grips my body tighter, and neither of us let go. We sob, letting ourselves feel the fear and sorrow of what is unknown, but what certainly lies ahead.

Soon, Joe's parents envelop the two of us tightly in their arms, our little family all together on that hard hospital bed. In a moment so raw, so scary, so unknown, we allow the silence to do the talking for us.

Joe, always the strong one, suddenly pushes us all away. Shocked, I look up questioningly at him. Attempting to compose himself, wiping his face and breathing deeply, he rests his elbows on his knees and lays his face in his hands. We wait impatiently—silently—for what is next.

What is the right word to describe being more scared than you thought possible? Not "frightened." Not "panicked." Not even "petrified." I never could find a word to describe it. My fear on the day of Joe's diagnosis was beyond anything I had ever experienced. I thought that the fear I felt that day could never be matched, but I was wrong, very wrong. Countless moments in the coming months and years far exceeded the fear I experienced on this worst day of our lives. The next few days would be even scarier than this day. Nights would be scarier than those days. And even when this part of our lives was over, I experienced fear that I could never have imagined that day. Nothing could have prepared me for the hell we were about to walk through.

Chapter 2

Our Love Story Begins

After years of fighting against the odds to escape the instability, dysfunction, and unfulfilled expectations of my childhood, I broke free. Emboldened by my own determination and a healthy dose of encouragement from several key adults—especially my high school basketball coach—I earned a full academic ride to a university near my small country town. Thirty minutes west, Missouri State University proved to be my new oasis—the place I would find hope, strength, and passion for my future.

I worked my first semester as a student-manager for the Missouri State University Lady Bears' basketball team. I loved it. Basketball had always played an important role in my life. In fact, as a high school student, it helped save me from a family life I loathed. Though I was no longer playing competitively, I knew leaving the game all together was impossible. This experience as a student-manager confirmed for me that someday I wanted to coach basketball.

After one semester, and no financial support from either parent, I decided to seek a full-time job. In the spring of my freshman year, I began working part-time as a customer service representative. Within eighteen months, I had been promoted three times. Working full-time, with a sixteen-hour course load each semester, proved incredibly challenging. It was a hectic, fast-paced life that involved little else than work, school, study, and sleep. I felt frustrated as I witnessed other students in my classes looking like they had just rolled out of bed after a crazy night of fun. I didn't get to go out to clubs and parties, or even to spend time with friends. I worked seven days a week, and I studied when I wasn't working. It didn't seem fair. Maybe it wasn't, but it did prepare me to be stretched beyond my physical and emotional limitations, a skill I was going to need again in just a few short years.

After my sophomore year of college, I ran into an ex-boyfriend's friend, Joe Smith. As they say, the rest is history. After exchanging numbers and pleasantries, we made plans to celebrate the Fourth of July by watching fireworks together in his hometown. We never spent another night apart. Joe was everything I had ever wanted: sensitive, sweet, caring. He had his own simple style—typically a white t-shirt and black cargo shorts. He had a crooked grin and a stay-to-himself, quiet personality—the opposite of mine. But he was confident in who he was and who I was, which helped me let go of my own insecurities. For the first time in my life, I felt loved unconditionally. He truly completed me. Like never before, I felt very full and very sure.

Joe and I moved in together after just a month of dating, sure of the future of our relationship from the beginning. We lived in Ridgedale, Missouri, about an hour from my school and work, which made for a long commute. Soon, the commute became taxing enough that I quit my job and began substitute teaching in a district close to home, where I was often placed in special education classes. As a criminology major, my senior project was on the methamphetamine problem in southwest Missouri. After spending time in these classrooms, I noted that many students were products of drug-induced homes and desperately needed positive role models. This experience planted in me a seed to someday become a teacher.

About a year after we started dating, we opened Joe's own mechanic shop at our home. We were anxious, not knowing if we would be successful since our home was so far off the beaten path. To our surprise, the business thrived!

On May 13, 2011, we celebrated my college graduation where I earned a Bachelor of Science in Criminology. My first job after graduating was working for the state of Missouri as an investigator of child abuse and neglect in our county. During my nine months on the job, I realized that though my job was to help children, I had very little time to directly influence the children I worked with. I decided that I wanted to change careers and become a special education teacher. Continuing my education, while accepting my first teaching job as an elementary special education teacher, I fell in love. God certainly created my heart to love big, and lead students. I knew I was doing exactly what I was supposed to be doing.

After two and a half years of dating, on January 7, 2012, Joe asked me to marry him. Coming up behind me, Joe presented me with my engagement ring, whispering, "Will you marry me?" I turned to face him and saw his bright blue eyes shining with excitement.

"Yes!" I exclaimed. Nothing could have made me happier.

Chapter 3

Mr. and Mrs. Smith:
Our First Year, Minus Nine Days

After a short, six-month engagement, the wedding day finally arrived. Joe and I packed up our truck and headed to a beautiful beach in South Carolina to start the next chapter of our lives. As we headed east, I could hardly contain my excitement: I was getting ready to marry the man I loved like no other—the one I wanted to spend the rest of my life with—on a beautiful summer evening at sunset on the beach. Could life get any happier than this?

We arrived in beautiful South Carolina and began preparations for the big day. Everything was low-key and stress-free. We were totally relaxed, focused on enjoying each other. As I walked barefoot onto the beach for the ceremony with my soon-to-be husband and a pastor to wed us, tears of happiness started to well in my eyes. As we vowed to join our lives together and sealed that vow with a kiss, my heart nearly exploded with happiness. The sun dropped below the horizon, the perfect conclusion to the day we became one.

After the ceremony, we enjoyed a celebration dinner, joyful bliss, and a goofy side I had never seen from Joe. Our photographer took the most beautiful shots—silly poses, many of them, but ones that captured our complete affection and pure joy. I had never been so happy as I was that day. This was the happiness I had yearned for my entire life. This was the marriage relationship I wished had been modeled to me, and now it was mine. At any moment, my heart could have burst out of my chest, and I was okay with it. I was now Mrs. Smith.

After our three-in-one wedding-honeymoon-summer vacation, we returned home. I had applied for a Temporary

Authorization Certificate and was hired as a special education teacher in my hometown, with the contingency that I complete special education classes and become a certified teacher. I would be coaching junior high school girls' basketball and teaching elementary special education. The only downside was the hour-and-twenty-minute commute. Though I loved the work, driving such a distance to and from school each day became stressful.

After my first semester of teaching and my twenty-fourth birthday, I became sick multiple days in a row. This illness felt different than other kinds of sickness I had experienced before. A pregnancy test confirmed our suspicions, and we excitedly planned for our upcoming arrival and our lives changing forever. I couldn't wait to meet our "little Joe," a boy who I was certain would be just like his daddy.

I finished out the school year at my alma mater, but I accepted a job for the upcoming school year in the district we lived in. I would get to continue to pursue my coaching and teaching career, only much closer to home. God knew what we needed—after all, a total of two hours and forty minutes in the car with a baby would be way too much. He certainly was looking out for us.

That may be the biggest understatement of our life—God was looking out for us. Our world was getting ready to crash, crumble, and fall out from beneath us. Our happily ever after wasn't going to be so happy. God knew way more than we did about what we were going to need. Before we had the faintest clue what our future would hold, God provided this job close to home. Over the next year, He continued to provide abundantly, beyond what anyone could have projected or foreseen. The truth is that God has a master plan, one that is unaffected by our best-laid plans.

Chapter 4

Unexpected

Summer vacation was here, and for an expectant mother who just wanted to sleep and not move, I could not have been happier. I even had no interest in enjoying beautiful Table Rock Lake, which is practically in our front yard. I only wanted comfort and bed. My pregnancy had been difficult, my face meeting the toilet bowl each morning before and after the shower. If I were lucky, I'd meet it only a few more times throughout the day. I was tired, and there was certainly no glow to my pregnancy, except for the beads of sweat rolling down my face every time I "lost my cookies."

My typically active husband spent plenty of time resting with me that summer, which I loved. He napped with me, or at least lay in bed next to me, running his fingers through my hair while relaxing and watching TV. He even had heartburn and gained weight like I did throughout our pregnancy. Our female friends and family giggled as they insisted, "That's normal. Joe is having sympathy pains like our husbands did."

The warm summer evening of June 18, 2013, Joe and I went for a visit to our best friends'—Jon and Nikki—home. Before even shutting the door, Joe's constant pain-in-the-butt friend, Jon, yells, "Dude, you look like shit!"

Laughing and knowing how these two operate, I rolled my eyes and strolled toward the air conditioning behind the front door. Joe played along, yelling back, "Thanks, man!" After all, it was dark, and with only the glow from the porch light, Jon couldn't tell what Joe looked like. Jon was serious, though.

He moved closer to look at Joe and said with some alarm, "No, man, seriously, do you feel okay? You look really yellow. Don't you think so, Nena?" Alarmed, I stopped mid-step and turned to study my husband's face. Choking up from the pregnancy hormones, I panicked at the sound of Jon's voice, the sincerity of his shock at the look of my husband. I, however, could not see anything unusual about the way Joe looked.

Realizing that Jon's usual brotherly joking was gone, I looked at Joe again and said, "I guess." I didn't mean it; I didn't see one thing wrong with him. He looked just the same as he always did. Upon entering their house, Jon continued his concerned rant and asked his fiancé, my best friend Nikki, what she thought about Joe's appearance. Nikki is the more practical-minded one, and the one I am more likely and willing to listen to. Nikki agreed with an alarmed look in her eyes, one that was scared, but guarded, because she knew I was seven months pregnant and prone to overreact, especially to things that involved Joe. Jon and Joe continued to fuss, and Joe acknowledged he had been really tired and had terrible heartburn lately, but that so had I since I had been pregnant.

Jon continued to rant about Joe's looking yellow and demanded he see a doctor. Joe and I wanted to wait on a doctor's appointment because we were in between insurance policies due to my change in school districts. We hesitated because we were attempting to live frugally. After all, we knew we would have lots of new expenses with a new son, whose arrival was expected in only two months. We found out sooner rather than later, though, that those baby-related expenses would be the least of our worries.

I believe God must have prompted Jon to overreact, to push, to be his persistent self to an extreme level that night. In hindsight, I know that Jon prolonged my husband's life.

I woke up the next day to a phone call from a local family physician's office, stating Jon had called to set up an appointment for Joe. The receptionist said I should be there June 20 at 3:30 p.m. with Joe in tow. Even though I could not see any change in him, I allowed my mind to wander to things unimaginable. Scared out of my mind, I ensured that Joe would be at this appointment, hoping it would rule out the worst of possibilities.

Fear of the unknown took over. I spent the next day sobbing in our bed, while Joe was off helping a friend build a shed in the blazing sun. His cell phone was out of service, so I couldn't reach him, magnifying the fears in my head and allowing the panic to set it. Then Joe called.

He told me he was on top of the roof of the two-story shed when he got dizzy: "I knew I couldn't make it down, so I held on to the rafters as tight as I could while lying on my belly. Babe, it was the weirdest thing. I threw up. Hard, I threw up really hard. The strangest thing was, my vomit was black and gray." My heart felt like it would shatter with worry.

"WHAT are you talking about, Babe? Did you fall? Where are you now? Are you okay? Do you think you just got overheated? Talk to me. Tell me what happened!" He couldn't because I couldn't stop asking questions.

Finally, stealing a moment while I took a breath, he muttered, "I don't know. I feel better now. But, Babe, it was the weirdest feeling I have ever felt. I can't explain it. I think I am just going to come home and eat a bowl of cereal and go to bed."

This statement should have registered as a loud, beeping alarm. Joe never came home and went straight to bed. Even so, I tried to explain away what had just happened to Joe. *It is hot today. He was up high on a shed, and he hates heights. It's probably all those things combined. Nothing is actually wrong, right? Because we are young and healthy and just married and expecting our first-born son together.*

Cue June 20, 2013. We had our seven-month pregnancy checkup. Our baby boy's heart rate was quick, more within normal range for a girl's heartbeat, but otherwise healthy and developing as expected. In all his years of treating expectant mothers, my doctor had never heard of anyone having pregnancy sickness this long. Constant reminders to eat bland foods, drink plenty of water, and ensure I ate high-calorie foods were repeated as we made our next check-up appointment.

After my doctor's appointment, we attended Joe's appointment. The doctor seemed nice enough as he went through his list of mundane questions. He agreed that Joe looked a little yellowish. "Have you noticed any blood in your stools?" he asked.

"No."

"Did you notice blood when you threw up the last time?"

"No."

"Anything seem abnormal?"

"Just tired, and I have heartburn. Occasionally the backs of my legs seem really fatigued, like I had just done leg workouts for days. Otherwise, no concerns, no other health issues—just excited to meet our son in two months."

The doctor handed over an at-home stool sample kit and drew blood to run some general tests. With a shake of his hand, he said, "I will call you tomorrow with the blood results."

He didn't, though.

He called fifteen minutes later.

We had just ordered our drinks at a local restaurant close to the doctor's office when my cell phone rang. I didn't know the number, but it was local.

"Hello?"

"Mrs. Smith?"

"Yes?"

"This is your husband's doctor. I already have your husband's blood results back. It is not good. I'm very concerned. A normal man's hemoglobin blood levels are between 12-14. A normal woman's hemoglobin blood count after giving birth typically falls between 8-9. Life threatening hemoglobin blood levels are a 6. Your husband's is a 4.7! Ma'am, I know you guys don't have health insurance, but you have to get him to a hospital immediately. I am direct-admitting him to Mercy Hospital in Springfield. You have to take him now; there is no option. They will have blood waiting for a blood transfusion. You have to get him there now!"

Whispering, trembling, shaking, quivering, I managed to choke out, "Okay."

Joe stared at me from across the table. Fighting the tears that were on the brim of my eyes, I couldn't seem to swallow the lump in my throat.

"Calm down," he said, as he unsuccessfully attempted to control my emotions.

"That was the doctor. He said to get to the hospital now."

"No! Geez, Babe, what did he say?"

I snapped and blurted out, "Yes, we are going!"

As the server approached, we routinely placed our order. I word-for-word repeated what the doctor had just told me.

"The doctor seems to be exaggerating the seriousness of this. I'm fine," Joe desperately concluded, attempting to convince himself. I think we both know I was convinced he was not at all fine.

Tense, irritated, and petrified, I demanded to get our food to go and be on our way. Alarmed, the server rushed to get our food and check as Joe began his protest of our evening schedule, insisting we go home first to grab a change of clothes and a quick shower. Joe won. His persistence was like nothing else I have experienced—bull headed, his way-or-no-way—yet he did it all calmly and subtly. I was angry and scared. Fighting tears and every what-if scenario that raced through my mind, I sat looking out the car window, wiping away tears as they streamed down my face.

"Joe, we are going straight to the hospital."

"Babe, we're going home to get some things and grab a shower."

Annoyed, attempting but failing to stay calm, I plead, "Please, it's just adding time on to us getting there. Something is wrong, and I am petrified for your life."

Once home, we showered, grabbed one outfit a piece and a few essentials; we planned on being gone for one night. We packed one small bag between us, and we were off to the most unknown adventure of our life. We were off to be introduced to our life for the next sixteen months. We did not speak a word. I am certain that every thought that was going through my head was also going through his.

Home. I should have savored every bit of the comfort of our home while we were there; I wouldn't see it for thirteen more days. Not my bed, not my clothes, not my anything. We would have a new home for thirteen days—Mercy Hospital.

Chapter 5

Entering the Unknown

We arrived at Mercy Hospital, entered through the large, loud emergency room doors, and approached the desk. Looking wide-eyed around the room, I heard many moans and groans, and I saw others wincing in pain. Nurses were moving busily behind the desk and looked eager to dismiss us.

"We're checking in for Joseph Smith," I piped up as Joe walked away from the desk in anxious pursuit of anything but this. The nurse looked at us over the computer, unamused by the joke she thought we were making by giving such a common name. Joe re-approached the desk, his face now serious and ready for business. She could not find us in the system. We reiterated our doctor's instructions, and with the help of another nurse, she finally found our name and order—fourth floor.

We followed the maze of large doors, wide corners, turns, and elevators and finally reached the fourth floor. Approaching the nurse's desk, we waited patiently for someone to assist.

"We're here to check in for Joseph Smith."

Looking up from her clipboard, the nurse said, "Oh, he has not checked in yet."

Joe and I looked at each other's face, questioning what she just said. I spoke up, "No, this is Joe Smith. We were told to come here to check in. The doctor direct-admitted us from Branson."

The nurse nearly flipped over the counter, as she looked down at Joe's feet, saw him standing, and looked back at his face. "You are standing. Wait, you are walking."

Looking at each other in confusion—and with increasing doubt that we should be treated at this hospital, with these nurses—I managed to respond, "Umm, yes, he is standing and walking. Are we in the right place?"

The nurse, with a complete astonishment that was still a mystery to Joe and me, hustled around and figured out where to send us—a shared room. We got settled quickly with the usual vitals, check-in, and questions. We then waited in uncomfortable silence for another three and a half hours, waiting on Joe's blood transfusion to begin.

"The plan is to do two bags of blood transfusions and to check your blood levels again. But the blood transfusions have to go slow, due to many reasons, and we will continually check-in on you during this time," the nurse shyly informed us. Her intentional lack of eye contact worried me, and I was certain she knew more than she was letting on.

We were further informed that Joe could not eat any of the food we had brought with us from the restaurant. I was starving and finally felt like I wouldn't heave my food up. I started to nibble, but I felt guilty. I knew Joe was as hungry as I was, but I couldn't resist. I took a bite to satisfy my stomach and my emotions. We watched TV to numb our minds and tried to ignore the silence between us. I could feel the fear we both shared and the constant, nagging lump in my throat.

While surviving an irritable roommate in the bed next to us, Joe received blood transfusions throughout the night. The next morning, Joe's hemoglobin blood levels had risen to a mid-eight level, but we were informed that still wasn't enough. A doctor requested at least two more units of blood transfusions and then a re-check on the hemoglobin levels to see if they had risen at all.

That next afternoon, Joe's hunger lingered. Chicken broth and Jello were all he was allowed. About two o'clock that afternoon, as the transfusions finished, Joe sat up on the side of the bed, and then stood. In a moment, Joe's face went from stark white to fleshy-pink, and then the color stretched the length of his body. It was the weirdest body-miracle I had ever seen. In awe, I half-gasped, half-whispered, "Are you okay? Your face, it just… it just flushed with color."

Smiling, he looked around with excitement, "Yeah!" he responded.

Boredom began to take a toll as we neared a full twenty-four hours confined to this tiny, sterilized room. Feeling trapped, we escaped to the hallway for a walk. Relieved at the sight of his feeling better, my nervous chatter took over the awkward silence that had numbed us both. The comfortable conversation returned, and I was certain the worst of our nightmare was over.

Wrong.

We were suddenly chased by a nurse back into our room where Joe was unhooked from his infusion. We were informed that his lab work would be repeated again even though his hemoglobin, we would later find out, was now registering in normal ranges for a healthy man.

More time passed as we waited for another physician to visit, who re-explained hemoglobin blood levels: "Although your hemoglobin blood levels have risen, we know that there is a place your blood must be going. It appears as if you are bleeding from the inside, and we need to figure out where that blood is going. This is the reason you have been feeling fatigue, possibly having heart burn, and the reason your blood levels have been dangerously low."

Astonished with the amount of information that this doctor poured out to us, Joe and I continued to nod with understanding.

"In order for us to figure out where the blood is going, we will need to do a colonoscopy and an endoscopy. Are you sure you have not seen blood in your stool or when you threw up?"

"I'm positive I have never seen blood."

"Okay. I will have a nurse come in and explain the prep you will need to do for us to get you into a colonoscopy first thing in the morning. Do you have any questions for me?"

A silent shake of his head, and darting eyes to avoid eye contact, Joe indicated the conversation was over.

"Good luck to you and your family."

The nurses came in with a gallon jug to inform us of the party that was about to ensue.

"Joe, you will need to drink the entire gallon of this clear solution that tastes awful but will clean you out. Pretty soon you will need to go the bathroom." Nodding his head with understanding, Joe reverted to his anxious, silent worrying; no words were exchanged between us.

"You will need to go to the bathroom" was an understatement. Joe returned to our hospital bed from his first visit to the restroom, "It felt like someone turned on a bathtub faucet the second I sat down to poop!"

The nurse reminded us, "Joe, you may need a commode bed side because it may be hard to make it to the toilet."

Joe refused. He refused very loudly, "I can control my own body and will not need a bed-side commode in front of my pregnant wife. She does not need to watch me go the bathroom all night long." Feeling his anger and frustration, the nurse and I exchanged quick glances, and she walked out of the room.

Joe sipped his lovely colonoscopy cocktail, and I gulped my fifteenth Dr. Pepper in the past two days. We were quiet, still, each searching for what news tomorrow would bring. The what-if game had started again. In hindsight, I should have known what was coming by the talk of "colonoscopy", "internal bleeding", and "low hemoglobin levels;" but I was oblivious, and my innocence masked the reality of what would be. I attempted to convince myself one more time, and so I repeated to myself, over and over and over again: *He's fine. There's nothing wrong. We will go home tomorrow, and everything will be okay.* Lying in that uncomfortable, hard recliner watching my husband's chest rise and fall for the rest of the night, I blinked out sleep in between his visits to the restroom.

Chapter 6

Reality

As I think back on the events of that morning—June 22, 2013—I am certain of this: Nothing can prepare you to learn that your husband has colon cancer. And nothing can ease the terror you feel nor the heartbreak you endure when you have to tell him the news yourself. We sat there numb, silent, waiting to wake up from this nightmare. But we never do.

I do not remember Joe's parents stepping out of the room. In fact, I do not remember anything other than lying in silence next to my sweet, sweet husband in that hospital bed, staring up at the western movie on TV. A tear hit my shoulder. I squeezed his left hand with my right. Neither of us looked at each other, knowing the tears were many, but our love was greater. A tear hit his hand, and he squeezed my hand tighter. I tried not to cry, but I failed miserably; my tears have a mind of their own.

Family and friends began showing up after a phone call to my elderly grandmother. My grandmother and uncles quickly arrived, attempting to stay strong for us. Later, my estranged mother and two brothers also appeared. Our tiny hospital room was tight, tense, and full of worry.

A tall, confident, short-and-to-the-point man entered our room. His green scrubs indicated he was the doctor we had been waiting on. This was the doctor who I had expected to tell my husband the worst news of his life, but who had left it to me. His confident ease and direct bedside manner immediately made me not like him at all.

"Hello, everyone. I'm Dr. B. You must be Mr. Smith?" Joe nodded his head. The lump was back in my throat. My eyes were wide, tears still sitting on the brims. And, again, I was more scared than I had ever been before. I grabbed Joe's hand, tighter.

"And you must be Mrs. Smith?" I nodded my head in agreement. "I am a colorectal surgeon here at Mercy. The doctor tells me they have found a cancerous tumor on your colon. What I need to do now is figure out family history." *Great*, I quietly thought to myself, *we are all here*.

Dr. B quickly stepped around and through everyone in the cramped room and made his way back to a small computer hanging on the wall in the right corner. He began typing in his credentials while still talking to us.

"Do you know of anyone in your family that has had colon cancer before?"

"Yes, my mom."

Joe's mom stepped forward and introduced herself. Dr. B never looked up at her from the computer but started listing off questions like a drill sergeant.

"How old were you? What side was it on? Did you do chemotherapy and/or radiation? How old are you now?" Joe's mom is as meek as she is small. Flabbergasted, she started rambling responses.

"Well, the first time I was, let's see, the first time I had endometritis cancer. I think I was…"

"WAIT! The first time? How many times are there?" the doctor demanded.

As she answered, Dr. B stopped typing. This very confident, to-the-point, I-am-in-a-hurry doctor, turned fully around, crossed his arms at his chest, and, without hesitation, interrupted her explanation.

"You are telling me you have had cancer three different times? The first time starting in your female parts, then two more times—both in the colon, once ascending and once descending, and you never once thought to tell your children they need to be tested ten years prior to the time you were originally diagnosed the first time?"

Joe's mom and dad looked at each other, astounded. Confused, she said, "I have never been told to do that."

Dr. B returned to typing, entering age of onset, what type of cancer she had and what type of treatment she received, as well as the medical history of her biological mother, Joe's maternal great-grandmother, and his maternal great-uncle. Then, all in one motion, Dr. B turned to me, interlaced his fingers, and said, "Well, this is certainly hereditary—Lynch syndrome. If this is as prevalent as the family history is showing, especially with the early age of onset, you need to have [pointing at my expecting tummy], boy, girl, whatever that is checked too because most likely they will have this as well."

Horrified and in shock, my mouth lingered open with no words coming out. Thoughts began bombarding my mind. I'd never in my life been so angry at someone for their lack of empathy.

"We have a few options here, Mr. Smith. One, we can take part of your colon. We can hope that the cancer is contained in that part of your colon, that it has not spread yet, and then you are good to go. Or, we can take your entire colon. From the sound of how prevalent your family history is, the chances of it coming back are pretty great. If we take your whole colon, there is no chance of the cancer coming back, or that it will spread throughout the colon again. Lucky for you, I am on-call this weekend, so we could get this surgery done tomorrow morning if you are interested."

Joe and I immediately caught each other's eye and stared at one other. We didn't say anything. We were scared to death. What was the right option, and how would we know? Neither of us said a word. Joe kept staring at my eyes. I wanted to tell him what I thought we should do, but I wasn't sure. Everyone in the room stared silently, searching back and forth between my husband and me, waiting for one of us to make a decision.

Dr. B saw our unease and uncertainty and broke the silence, "I mean, you do not have to make a decision immediately. We can get you back in here, start another round of drinking the good stuff for the colonoscopy, then go through with the surgery at a later time."

I immediately disagreed. Words started flowing, "Well, there is a rush. I am seven months pregnant, and I need him to be healthy and good when our baby gets here."

Joe blurted out, "What happens if I have the whole colon removed? Would I have to wear a colostomy bag?"

"No," the doctor answered. "I would be able to attach the very end of the intestine directly to the rectum. The only difference in using the bathroom would be instead of going one or two times a day, you would use the bathroom three or four times a day."

Joe and I stared, again, right into each other's eyes. "Babe, I think we need to do this now. Your mom, she's had it so many times already; it keeps coming back. We cannot go through this again. We cannot do another surgery with a baby. Let's just make sure it all gets out. Nothing to worry about after this."

Joe respected my opinion on nearly every topic, and this one was no different. He didn't say another word but looked at me with the final decision on his face.

Dr. B continued to look back and forth between us as we stared at each other, trying to get confirmation we wanted to go through with the surgery. He took our silence as confirmation and continued, "Okay, well, we will plan for surgery in the morning. You will be my third case, so between nine and ten. The nurses will get you prepped and tell you what you need to do before they bring you down to the surgery floor. Do you have any questions for me?"

We continue to stare. *Yes,* I thought to myself, there are a thousand questions. We both knew all of them. *Will he be here for the birth of our son? Will everything go back to normal again after this? This will save his life, right? Oh, and how dare you have no bedside manner when you just told me to make sure I have my unborn, whatever it is, checked for cancer too.*

"No, no questions."

"Okay, great. I will see you all in the morning."

Signing off the computer, he shook my hand and Joe's as well. Half-smiling at everyone in the room, our surgeon pushed his way out, and I heard him barking orders at the nurses' station in the hallway.

Dying inside, I wanted everyone to leave so I could just look at my husband. As if on cue, many of our family members started filing out to the hallway while others said their good-byes. After hugs of comfort and plans made for tomorrow, I visited the public bathroom right outside our hospital room. Alone, I sprawled out on that nasty, disgusting, public bathroom floor and bawled. I cried and screamed some more. Then, I splashed my face with water, swallowed that constant lump in my throat, and went back to our hospital room to be with my husband.

As we held on to each other for comfort, we received countless phone calls of love and concern. Late that night, while preparing for the morning that lay ahead of us, a number I did not recognize popped up on my phone. It was a voice from my past.

"Hello?"

"Nena?"

"Yes."

"It's Dad."

Silence.

"Are you there?"

Sitting on the floor, legs crossed, sobbing and nodding my head yes, I could only respond with silence.

"Nena, are you there?"

"Yeah. Yeah, I am here," I said, choking back all the day's emotions.

"I just heard your husband has been diagnosed with cancer. Is that right?"

"Dad, I need you. I need you really bad."

"I know you do. What's going on?"

I tell him, in detail, the chain of events that have transpired the past two days.

Despite my need for comfort from my parent, my father quickly shifted the conversation from the current crisis to a diatribe on the past. The history of my family's relationships is full of hurt, accusations, misunderstandings, and anger. It is a mess.

But being just hours away from my husband's cancer diagnosis and upcoming total colectomy was not the time to be having this conversation. And so, looking at Joe, the man who truly mattered, I ended the phone call abruptly.

I hung up and cried. I realized in this moment how much I still needed my father, even with everything that had transpired between us. Yet, he was unable to be there for me in my vulnerable state. This broke my heart. I stood up to join Joe in our hospital bed. Suddenly in pain, I screamed and clutched my stomach. Joe bolted out of bed and rushed to my side as I hunched over, hanging on to the window's edge. Attempting to hold me upright, Joe kept pleading, "What? What's wrong? Babe, talk to me! What is wrong?"

Gasping for air, I managed, "I don't know. I...I think, I think these are contractions!" Continuing to huff and puff, I allowed Joe to help me down into the uncomfortable hospital recliner. I winced, the pain in my swollen belly and pelvis excruciating. Trying to concentrate, I told this little boy inside of me that Daddy needed me right now, so he would have to wait to make his appearance.

In that moment, I discovered something about myself I could never believe before. When faced with overwhelming fear and despair, I did not have to succumb. I had the ability to stay calm. I didn't have to overreact and get worked up. I couldn't. My husband needed me, and for me to take care of him, I had to keep my body calm for our son—even when I felt beyond petrified. There was no fixing this. I could not control this. I took a deep breath, knowing this journey would probably require more of me than I had to give. But this wasn't about what I needed; this was about what our son and my husband needed, and I knew that God would never leave me and would always give me the strength to handle whatever came next.

We did not sleep again that night. How would you, knowing you were going in for a surgery to lose one of your organs? I constantly repeated silent prayers through the night, *Please, God. Let this be it. Let him be alive for the arrival of our son. Do not let me do this alone. Will you let him be here for his first Christmas? Please God! I am begging you. Let this be the healing he needs. Let us have his life back. I'll never forsake you again.* Over and over and over again, I begged God. I knew I had never believed in Him more than I did in this moment. I never needed Him more than I did in this moment. I was angry at Him, but I also praised Him because I knew He was our only answer, our only hope. And then I cussed Him for letting this happen.

Joe kept his glasses on, with his eyes closed. He was not asleep—I knew that. All night long, I watched his chest rise and fall over and over again. I noticed how normal he looked; he didn't even look sick! All night long I played what-if with myself again. I silently cried and turned over to my other side, taking my eyes off him for short periods of time. I wiped my silent tears, swallowed hard that lump, and rolled back over to watch him. Rise and fall. Rise and fall. *Christmas? Thanksgiving? Any pictures together? Labor by myself?* Tears, looking away, wiping them away, watching—I repeated this all night. Lab people came in and out a few times to draw more blood. He opened his eyes, smiled, hugged me, and reminded me to go to sleep. I smiled back. I kissed him at least five hundred times that night. I did not sleep.

Chapter 7

Surgery

5:21 a.m. I heard a small voice whisper, "The doctor has changed his plan. You are going to be his first case this morning. We need you to get up and take a shower with the anti-bacterial soap. Make sure to scrub really well to avoid any infection during the surgery."

I was up. Straight up. Hustling around, packing that extra outfit I had already worn twice. Pulling my hair straight back, brushing my teeth. Joe sat on the edge of the bed. He had not eaten in three days. He was hungry. He was tired. He was scared. I knew he was thinking and feeling many things, but he did not—would not—tell me. He would start crying if he did. I could not stop moving around. I wanted to fix this. Only, there was no fix.

"Babe, come on. You need to get in the shower. Let's go. I don't want us to be late."

"Just give me a minute. I am trying to wake up. And you are over there acting like you are running a marathon."

I laughed. I needed to. It was true, though. When I am nervous and anxious, I can't sit still.

I sat next to him and grabbed his hand. We both looked at the floor. "Are you scared?"

How stupid was that for me to ask my husband. I knew him better than he knew himself. Duh, he was scared.

"Well...yeah. I just, how do we know if we made the right decision? I mean, what if we make the wrong one?"

That, I did not know. Again, I didn't have answers, and I could not fix this. And I sure didn't like it. Trembling, I replied, trying to be confident, "I don't know. I think we made the right choice, though." I said this, but I didn't know if I believed my own words.

Joe shook his head, stood up, and turned away from me. I knew he was crying and that he didn't want me to see. He walked to the shower, shut the door. He knew that the shower was the safest place to escape to if he didn't want me to see him cry.

I called his mom and dad to tell them the surgery would be earlier. They hadn't slept either but would be right up. Joe's mom was talking frantically and said Joe's dad hadn't said a word, only sobbed. "Me too," I choked out. "Me too." She said some family was coming up, so she would call to let them know about the earlier time. Secretly, I just wanted to be by myself with Joe. No one else. I wanted to be selfish and hog every last second with him. I couldn't. They wouldn't let me. God wouldn't let me do this by myself.

Joe emerged, fresh and clean, his eyes free of tears. I swallowed the lump in my throat and willed my tears to stop. Courtesy hospital bags sat on our hospital bed, full of the extra outfit we each had, empty of hope. The nurse came in and asked if we were ready. "Yes," said my quivering voice. *No!*, screamed my trembling body.

The hallways were quiet. It was only 5:43 in the morning. Soon, life would be abundant, loud, and chaotic in all these hallways. Joe sat quietly in a wheelchair as they pushed him toward the surgery wing. I quickly waddled right beside him, every few seconds glancing over to see his face. It was the same every time— his solid, stone-cold face stared straight ahead. We finally made it to the check-in location. Not one volunteer was behind the information/check-in desk yet. The nurse told me this desk was where I could get updates on Joe throughout surgery. She then showed me the waiting rooms right next to it. Chairs, chairs, and more chairs. TVs, magazines, electrical outlets to recharge devices—conveniences intended to derail the stress, confusion, and worry while we waited. But not one of them soothed me or gave me what I wanted.

The nurse informed me I would need to wait there since Joe would soon move into pre-op. The anesthesiologist and other doctors would check in with him, and nurses would check his vitals until the surgery team arrived and was ready to perform the surgery. I stood there blankly batting my eye lashes in defense of the tears that were welling up and getting ready to surge down my face. My eyes were burning.

I don't know why, but that nurse allowed me to break the rules that day. Maybe it was my seven-month swollen tummy, maybe it was the haunting fear in my eyes, maybe it was the silent screams coming from Joe's eyes, maybe it was our interlaced hands obviously trembling, or maybe it was the sheer emptiness of the waiting room. Whatever the reason, she offered, "You know what, no one is here yet—you are the first. Why don't you come back with him until he is ready to be wheeled into surgery."

For a moment, my heart did not feel squeezed up into my throat, and my tears stopped. I followed the nurse and Joe through the white double doors and back to the pre-operation room. Bed after bed after bed, as far as I could see. They all looked identical, with the same machines next to them, the same folded and tucked sheets from end-to-end. It was a scary sight. The nurse pointed to Joe's designated bed, and he slipped in. The nurse wished us the best of luck and informed another nurse we had made our arrival. The new nurse smiled warily when she saw us—a young couple, scared out of their minds, with an ever-growing belly between them. Joe was still quiet. The nurse introduced herself and begged me to sit on a stool that she swore she could find somewhere. I obliged when it was delivered to Joe's bedside and offered to me.

My strong, creative, always-in-charge husband was still quiet. And I was too. My mind raced with, *What could I say?* Nothing. There was nothing to say. I was scared, angry, petrified—whatever word could actually describe the feeling that I was going to die because of the fear in my bones. We were both feeling that at this moment. I could not stand the beeping of machines and the nurses and doctors coming in and out.

I told Joe his parents were on their way. He still didn't look at me. "Okay," he replied. He stared at his lap, covered by a white, rough, hospital blanket. I stared at him, examined every inch of his face—his big ears, his shaved head, his glasses. I moved my gaze down to his strong arms, his calloused hands, and that one thing that represents we belong together—his wedding ring. I blurted out, "Do you want me to take your ring?" He nodded. He brought his left hand up to his face, sliding that shiny tungsten circle around and around a few times on his finger as he examined it closely. All I wanted to hear was whatever his mind was thinking. Instead, he slowly slid his ring off and handed it to me while he looked the other way. I was certain I was about to die from holding the tears in so long. I death-gripped that shiny thing that I never knew meant so much to me.

An anesthesiologist approached and introduced himself. He asked Joe his birthday—a question it seemed he'd answered one hundred forty-two times since we'd been at that hospital—and if he knew what surgery he was about to have. Joe replied robotically, in monotone. The doctor half-smiled at me. I was getting used to that response. I slowly laid my head in Joe's lap with my gaze away from his face and toward his blanket-covered feet. I didn't know what I was trying to do, think, say, wonder, believe. I just knew that, right then, my body on his was the safest place on Earth, and I was getting ready to be pulled away from it.

The surgeon who we'd met the day before, Dr. B, approached through the sliding door. Chipper, confident, and aloof—the opposite of my emotional state—he repeated the questions the anesthesiologist had just asked. Joe replied. I watched my lover's mouth move as the words came out. I stared blankly, blinking back the tears. I did not want the time to come for the doctor to tell me to leave, to wait, without Joe in my immediate sight. He told us the laundry list of possible side-effects of this surgery, but all I heard was "possibility of death." I nearly fainted.

Blinking and batting my eyes were not enough to stop the tears from rolling down my pale face. Dr. B looked at me and said, "I promise to take good care of him. I will come talk to you after we finish up. It should take no longer than five or six hours." I think I nodded, but no words would come out.

Joe exhibited no emotion. I hated his not talking, not responding, not giving me any visual of what he was thinking. Though I am sure I knew what he was thinking, I wanted to hear it from his mouth. But then I remembered I couldn't fix it. All I wanted to do was to wake up from this nightmare. It couldn't be real.

The nurse approached again. "It is time. The surgery team is here, and they are ready to take you back." She glanced at me, then away, then at Joe, then back at me, then to the floor. I knew she was hinting that I should go to the waiting room. My mind raced. *I need to be strong. He doesn't need to see me scared and upset. It will only upset him more. What can I say or do to prolong my leaving the room? Act quickly. Think of something.*

"Mrs. Smith, we will come out to get you once the surgery is done. If you have any questions, you can ask at the desk you saw when you were first brought in. They can contact us back in the operating room. If something comes up, then we will let the desk know, and they can inform you."

I looked up and noticed many more people had filled the simple beds all the way down the room. However, no other spouses or loved ones stood near them. I felt for those lying in those beds—alone. Then, I realized Joe would be alone too, in just a few seconds. My tears were falling; his tears were brimming at his eyes now too. I leaned over, with our unborn son in between us, to hang onto his neck— not to let go. He wrapped me up tightly—not to let go. I could feel his tears on my shoulder, and I knew he could feel mine on his too. I was deathly afraid right then, and the only person in my life who had shielded me from pain, loneliness, and debilitating fear couldn't shield me any longer. I whispered, "I love you" and squeezed him tighter. He repeated the same to me. I willed that moment to never end. I couldn't unlock my arms from him. I couldn't move. Like a stone statue, we remained there, physically still, but I was actively begging God for my family's life.

I don't remember how I stood up or let go. I remember looking away, then immediately down to our things, picking them up and trying to wipe away my tears in an attempt to conceal that I was a hysterical, sobbing mess. I could not. I looked back at him and grabbed his large hands. I stared at his fingers, at his perfectly square nail beds, and told him again, "I love you. I love you so much. I'm going to see you in just a few hours. I'll be right outside those doors—just right outside. I promise I won't be far away." I was crying, desperately trying to reassure myself that it was all going to be fine. Joe squeezed my hand tightly, leaned his shaved head back on the pillow and closed his eyes. Tears were still falling down his cheeks.

How do I walk out and let him go? I still need to say things. I need to watch this surgery. What if they do something wrong? Isn't there an observation room like you see on TV where people are looking through the glass at the surgery table and doctors? Why didn't they recommend for me to get to sit there? What if they need me? What if Joe needs me? I didn't know what to do, and my body was frozen in fear. The nurse must have sensed this and came up behind me to show me where to walk out. I kept looking back. *Is he okay? Babe, just tell them you need me, okay? What if we just waited a few more minutes? I could stay just a bit longer.*

No, I could not. I yelled out at the last glimpse of him, "I love you, Baby!" Then, I was through the sliding doors and immediately out the double doors. Joe's mom and dad were standing right there at the large, oak corner desk. I told myself, *Don't you dare; don't let it go. Joe needs you. Be strong.*

Joe's mom tried to be happy, warm, reassuring, "Hey, there you are." I had been strong too long the past few days. I kept it together in front of him. I couldn't anymore. I began to fall to my knees, tears flooding my face and down to my shirt. Joe's dad caught me, put his arm around me, and forced me to walk to a chair. And I sobbed. I sobbed and sobbed and screamed, begging God to comfort me and to save my husband.

I remember little else, other than a calm, sweet, elderly woman coming up to me with a navy-blue Mercy vest on. She informed me I could check on my husband's progress on a large, flat-screen plasma television that hung on the wall. She gave me a cheat sheet with a chart of various colors that each indicated a different part of the surgery process. She also told me to come ask any questions I might have. All I knew was the five minutes Joe had been out of my sight felt like the entire six hours he was supposed to be in surgery.

When I looked up, I noticed one of the four sections of the waiting room was full of familiar faces—Joe's family. His aunts, uncles, cousins, second cousins, paternal grandmother, mom, dad, his parents' best friends were waiting right there with me. They stared back at me, not knowing what to say; but the looks in all their eyes were of confidence. I didn't know what I was supposed to say or do, so I cried. And I hugged every single one of them. I looked around again at the waiting room overflowing with our friends and family, a testament to how much we are loved. I knew this was true, yet in the moment, it did not encourage me.

Eventually, Joe's family, looking concerned, asked me if I'd eaten anything. I had not. I was not about to leave that waiting room, where I was the furthest distance from Joe I had been since the diagnosis. But trying to fight with my husband's family, the only people more stubborn and strong-willed than me—these people were a force!—didn't work. I reluctantly decided to go eat something in the cafeteria. That ham-mozzarella-mushroom omelet sat on my plate staring back at me as I continued to try to choke back tears, and failed.

I laid my head on the table while twenty family members stared at me, trying to console me. The buzzer I had been given in case the doctor needed to alert me went off. I jumped to my feet and began to waddle-run my seven-month pregnant self to the elevators. This was exactly why I didn't want to leave the waiting room in the first place. I made it to the check-in desk and showed them my buzzer; the volunteers confirmed it was just to let me know they had taken Joe back into surgery. My heart racing, somewhat more relieved and more devastated, I slumped into a chair. Joe's family started to trickle back in to the waiting room, whispering to each other what the lady at the desk had told me.

The hours it took to complete Joe's surgery seemed like an eternity. I paced, walked, and constantly checked the television chart to see what stage of the surgery they were in. It never changed. I ran over in my head again and again what the nurses had said: *About five to six hours.* I decided I would give it six hours and twenty minutes; then, I would check in with the desk. The sixth hour and twentieth minute came. I was sick, yet I was pacing faster than I thought possible with my swollen belly. I was sweating. Crying. Fidgeting. *What could have gone wrong?* The grandmotherly volunteer said she would call back to the surgery room to check. I could barely stand waiting for the response.

Instead of a call back, a nurse came from the surgery room to find me. "All is well," she said. "We just ran into a few things we were not expecting. We should be finished up soon." Got it. He's good. It's okay. Our nightmare would be over after this.

About a half hour later, Dr. B quickly stepped out of those double doors to find me. He sat me down away from everyone else in the waiting room and shook my hand.

"All went well in there. I need to apologize because I really thought I could get Joe's entire colon out laparoscopically. We got through the entire surgery great, and then I got to the final part where the tumor was, and I tugged, pulled, and played—but the tumor was too large to get out. Right at the very end of the entire surgery, I ended up having to cut him all the way open to get the tumor out. His incision is pretty large down his abdomen, and he will be in a lot of pain. Had we known from the beginning that we would have to cut him open, we would have given him an epidural for the pain. Now we will have to play catch up with the pain."

Hesitantly, yet firmly, I replied, "Please do not apologize for taking cancer out of my husband's body. Thank you for ridding him of this. I just want to see him, please."

Dr. B told me that Joe was in holding and would be taken to his recovery room shortly. He explained the pain pump he would be on, but that the recovery nurses would let me know more. I shook his hand, and in that moment, I had never been so thankful for anyone in my entire life. I was surprised I felt this way given his less-than-tactful bedside manner the day before. But that day, Dr. B impressed me, and I chose to be thankful for his part in our story, that God had put him in our path to extend Joe's life, and the life of our family.

Chapter 8

Post-Surgery

Waiting to see Joe was an eternity. I was anxious, nervous, trying to understand what to expect. More friends. More family. Some left, some stayed. None knew what to do, but I heard the whispers, "Has she eaten? Did she sleep? Will she just rest, do you think?" I ignored all of them. Over my dead body was I about to shut my eyes or be anywhere away from my husband. Then I heard Joe's dad's voice, "Nena." I spun around and stared into his eyes; he pointed at the double doors. Joe.

I ran to the hospital bed. He was motionless, flat on his back, eyes shut. His forehead was furrowed, his eyes winced, his mouth released moans of pain. I thought I might die; I could not bear to see him like this. I yelled, "I am right here, Baby; it's me. I am right here. I'm not going anywhere." I hoped this might help the pain, but of course it wouldn't. I was helpless. Realizing this fact was the most challenging part of our journey. I could not fix it. I couldn't do one damn thing to make any of it go away. And I couldn't stand it. I was completely helpless to make things better for my husband—my best friend, my soulmate, the father of our unborn son. This is the lesson I still cannot accept to this day. It has ravaged my soul.

The nurses pushed Joe's bed down the labyrinth of hallways to his room—our home for the next twelve days. The nurses asked me to stay in the hall so they could transfer him into the other bed. I reluctantly agreed. All I knew was I was about to flip out if I didn't get to touch him, hold him, and run my hands over the shaven, prickly hairs on top of his head. When they shut the door, I turned around. The sea of family and friends had followed. I felt trapped, kept away from the only thing I wanted, and my inner anguish and frustration were building.

The nurses finally emerged from the room, and I leapt through the door frame. The moans—so loud. His forehead furrowed, eyes still winced shut. I hunkered down, careful not to hurt him, and put my lips on his right ear. I whispered as quietly as possible, "You made it. You did great. I love you so much! We are going to get through this. I promise. You did amazing. It is all gone! Dr. B got it all. I know it. It's going to be good from here on out. We are going to get through. Oh, Baby, I love you so much!"

I am not sure if I was telling him this to reassure him or saying it out loud so I would believe it myself. Maybe both. Joe's parents and grandma walked in. They showered Joe with their I-love-yous, it's-going-to-be-okays, and we-are-proud-of-yous. Joe only moaned back.

Joe's mom begged me to eat. I didn't want anything except Joe. I needed him. I needed to touch him, to see him, to be with him. I sat next to the hospital bed with my right hand in his. I lowered my forehead on top of our united hands. And I wept. I wept long and hard, begging God that the tears streaming down my face were enough of a prayer since, in that moment, I had no words to pray. One hundred thousand thoughts were spinning through my head. I was begging God for mercy, grace, anything that would save our life together.

A nurse interrupted. She explained the pain pump, how it would light up when Joe was allowed to have another dose of pain medicine. She attempted to wake Joe. He opened his eyes and shut them immediately. She informed me the oxygen mask under his nose was connected to the pain pump. The pain pump would sound a loud alarm if he was not breathing enough breaths per minute—necessary because of the strength of pain medications he was being given. I shook my head in astonishment and uncertainty. Got it. Check. She asked if there was anything I needed. "No," was my response, but "My husband to be perfectly healthy" was the real answer.

She started for the door, turned around and said, "You should probably rest. It looks like you need it." I politely gave a half-smile and nodded.

The door shut, and Joe barely eked out, "Babe." I jumped up, hovering over him.

"Hey. There you are. I love you. The surgery went good." I kissed his forehead, rubbed his whiskery hair on top of his head. I smiled, tears streaming down my face, kissed his head again.

"How's my boy in there?" Joe asked, pointing to my belly. I thought my emotions would overtake me before I could answer his selfless question.

"He is fine. Don't you worry about him. We just need you to get to feeling better so he has his daddy," I choked out in fragmented pieces.

Joe didn't talk much the rest of the day. He was still heavily sedated. I don't remember a lot of that afternoon except that I was always touching Joe. I remember his touch to my skin. I'll never forget it. And tears, constant tears. Panic, fear, and that whatever-is-beyond fear feeling.

Our friends—John, Shaun, and Nikki—arrived later that evening for a visit. Our friends surrounded the bed and woke Joe up. Jon checked the machines and tubes around Joe's bed like he was his doctor and rubbed Joe's head like he was in love with him. Shaun added to the bromance by rubbing Joe's feet. These grown men could not stop razzing each other, even there in the hospital room. They are like brothers—loving, worrying, supporting, and wanting to fix this for their friend, for his family. I watched and laughed inside. I felt happy that we had people who loved us so much—family that was chosen, closer than our own blood. They eventually left and promised Joe they'd return and that they would take care of me.

The rest of the evening stayed busy with family saying their good-byes, whispering their I-love-yous, reminding me they would do anything I needed. I knew there was nothing to ask for. I half-smiled, said thank you, and lied that I would call if I needed anything.

After nearly everyone left, Joe's parents again begged me to eat. Joe's mom asked if I had eaten at all. Staring with concentration, I nodded my head yes, but quickly corrected myself, "No, I haven't." Someone delivered half of a turkey sandwich on white bread. I devoured it. *I could use another one of those*, I thought to myself. Before I knew it, I had more in front of me to eat.

I don't remember much more about that night except for one hospital staff member asking me every time she was in our room if *I* needed anything. Even though I was sleep-deprived, un-showered, physically uncomfortable, and emotionally spent, my answer was always no; in my mind, all I needed was my husband to be okay. But those around me knew better. They worked to take care of me when I wouldn't take care of myself.

Chapter 9
Life Alarm

I didn't think I could be more physically, mentally, or emotionally exhausted than I was that night after everyone left. The night nurse re-explained to me that because of the high doses of pain medication Joe was still on, he needed to wear the oxygen mask that would measure his breathing and ensure his respiratory system didn't shut down. In other words, they needed to prevent him from dying from the amount of pain medication he was on. She reminded me the machine would sound an alarm if he was not taking enough breaths. I was scared to death.

I pulled up the most uncomfortable recliner known to man next to Joe's hospital bed. He was out of it, but I am sure he knew I was right there because I never stopped touching him to make sure he was okay. After piling pillows on each side of me, behind me, and on top of me, I was as comfortable as I was going to get. I dozed off for maybe ten minutes before the alarms started. I panicked and shook Joe awake, reminding him to take some deep breaths. I felt under his nose, on his chest, and in front of his mouth to make sure he was still breathing. He was. This scene repeated itself for the next ten hours, no more than five minutes between each alarm.

Joe was upset, frustrated, and angry because he needed to sleep—both physically and because of the medicine. I was too scared to sleep. The pillows I had so carefully arranged were forgotten. I was now sitting leaned over the bed, my forehead resting on the sheets while I held Joe's hands. As soon as I heard the alarms go off again, I jerked up, gripped his hands, and shook his arms, desperately trying to remind him to breathe. Eventually, a nurse told us she was certain the machine was broken and finally agreed to exchange it for another one. But the other one sounded no less often.

I was so tired I couldn't stop crying. I could feel my eyelids hanging halfway down my eyeballs, and my body was begging me to lie down and rest. As morning approached, the day nurse entered our room, and I explained what kind of night we had had. She made an executive decision to take the machine off, shut our door, and post a sign on it that demanded no one enter. She told me to sleep and to let Joe sleep. We followed her orders.

I remember waking up, looking at my phone, and realizing we had slept four hours straight. I felt like a new person.

Chapter 10

Recovery Days

Our recovery days were busy with visitors. Many people stopped by to pray with us, to let us know they were thinking of us, or to deliver food, drinks, and gifts to brighten our days. Joe stayed asleep most of the time, as the pain medication was still being administered in extremely high doses. He would partially wakeup, give me his signature half-smile when he saw my face, and then fall right back to sleep.

I felt like a story teller as I repeated to everyone who asked the circumstances that led us to this hospital room. Months later Joe told me that during those recovery days, even with his sedated mind, he could hear my telling everyone the same story over and over. Most everyone cried with me, hugged me, and told me they would do whatever I needed. But what I needed, they couldn't provide, so I didn't ask for help.

What I needed was security that despite our small business not running because Joe was in a hospital bed and despite the hospital bills that I knew would be beyond any amount we could ever re-pay, we would have a home to live in, food to eat, and all the things we needed for our new baby on the way. What I needed was a promise that my husband was going to be okay. What I needed was someone to deliver a miracle—that Joe would be completely cured and would be there not only for the birth of our son, but for every single birthday and Christmas. I needed someone to tell me this was all a sick lie and I could wake up any time. That nightmare cliché made sense now—this could not possibly be my life and yet, it was.

In between visitors, a familiar social worker stopped by our room. I had had a discussion with her a couple of days prior in which she had requested bank statements, tax returns, and other financial information that I promised I would get to her as soon as we got home. I hadn't been home yet. As she entered our room the second time, her voice shaky, she said, "So, I guess things are a lot worse than what we originally thought, huh?" I stared blankly at her because that didn't even begin to explain how different all of this was than what we had thought.

I knew in my heart the social worker was just doing her job, but this was not the time I needed to discuss finances or how we would never be able to pay back the medical bills we have now, much less those we would continue to incur. She began asking questions about property values, car values, bills we had, income coming in. The lump in my throat didn't allow me to speak, and the anger of even having to discuss any of this infuriated me. The tears were streaming slowly down my face.

After every one of her questions, I answered, "You can take my house; you can take everything in it. As long as I have him lying by my side every night, there is nothing else I need." Upon hearing my response, this attractive, young professional closed her book, glanced down, and then looked back up at me with tears in her eyes. She said she understood and gave me her card. She told me whenever we got home to send her the information she requested.

I remember thinking how angry I was at Joe—angry that he was lying there sleeping when I, his seven-months-pregnant wife, could not seem to sleep at all; angry that he wasn't worrying about finances because he was, instead, lying there in a pain medication-induced fog. I was angry that the burden of all of this was on me. In the very next moment, though, I knew that was a lie.

In my despair, it looked like he had it easier, but I knew in my heart that I did. My husband wanted to give the best life to me and to our son. I couldn't imagine the helplessness he felt lying there, powerless to do anything to ease the burden this diagnosis put on me and our family. I snapped out of my despair and resolved to do what I could to ease the burden this diagnosis put on him.

Joe's parents came back up to the room with clean clothes, pillows, and comfort things from home—Joe's blanket, a hoody, my computer. Finally, for the first time in four days, I took a shower. Although everyone begged me to go across the street to shower at a cousin's apartment that we could see from our hospital window, I was not going to be away from him. I took that shower in Joe's hospital bathroom. It was one of the most magnificent showers I've ever taken in my life. Like Joe had discovered before his surgery, I realized then what a sanctuary the shower would become for me. It was a place where I could sob without anyone, especially Joe, seeing or hearing me. I changed into fresh clothes and brushed my teeth. I felt renewed, like I might be able to tackle something important that day, like I had a little more fight. Thank goodness because I was going to need a lot of fight for the next sixteen months.

After everything we'd been through those past few days—the diagnosis, the surgery, the finances, the social worker—I knew one thing for certain. It really is true that money or circumstances cannot buy happiness. None of what society tells us we need to be happy—to look a certain way, to obtain material wealth, to gain power or status—produces the kind of happiness I felt in that hospital room that day. And even years later, still nothing compares.

Chapter 11

Something is Wrong

Somehow, I was sleeping soundly on the ply-board couch until our doctor and nurses entered our room for 6:00 a.m. rounds. Completely disoriented, I jumped straight up (as I had every other time a nurse came in Joe's room that night to check vitals or draw blood) and stared at them, trying to figure out where I was and why these people were looking at me.

Dr. B announced that today was the day Joe needed to get up and walk. Upright, but still half asleep, I raised my eyebrows to force my eyes open. I repeated what he just said, but with a question mark in my voice. Didn't he know Joe had basically slept the past three days since surgery and had not moved from his bed? Didn't he realize that a huge machine still controlled his pain medication and that he would need to stay hooked up to that? How could he possibly walk? Dr. B empathetically looked at me and said, "It's called tough love; you'll have to have some."

Choking back tears, I continued to stare at him as he lingered. He had more information to share. Looking towards the door, back at Joe, and then hesitantly at me, he said, "The results came back from the biopsy of the part of the colon they removed; the pathology report shows the cancer is in the lymph nodes. They are classifying this as stage III colon cancer." Somewhere in the far-off distance I heard him say something about our needing to meet with an oncologist to begin a chemotherapy plan to ensure all cancer is killed. "Treatment will need to begin about a month after surgery, and you need to be ready to speak with doctors to make a plan." He said they would send someone in later. I truly felt like there was nothing else that could go wrong. He looked at me hesitantly, yet perfectly in command, then turned around and walked out.

I slowly lowered myself back onto the most uncomfortable bed I've ever had the pleasure of sleeping on. I thought out loud, "Dr. B is out of his mind."

Not knowing Joe was awake, let alone alert enough to know what was just said, I heard a "Yep!" from his bed. I smiled because we were still on the same page. I knew full well, though, that if the doctor thought a walk was the next step in the plan to save my husband's life, I would attack the plan.

The walk did not need to be far, just past four hospital room doors and back, just one time that day. I was scared to death to try to get Joe up and walking. What if he wasn't strong enough? What if *I* wasn't strong enough? Joe told me there was no way he could do it. I wanted to agree with him, but I didn't. I just promised him I would be right there with him to get him up and walking. By early afternoon, I had reminded him at least six times that he needed to get up and walk.

Aggravated with my constant reminders, he opened his eyes to say, "I know, Babe, just give me some time to rest. I am exhausted." I am sure he wanted to put his hand over my mouth.

After some time, I repeated it again, "Babe, we have to get up and walk."

He responded again with the same disgusted, annoyed voice, only much more frustrated this time, "I know!"

At about the end of my patience, I said, "I'll let you sleep another hour, but then we are getting up to do this. And then it will be over. I won't bother you any more today, but we have to get this done."

Joe still had his eyes closed. In response to my ultimatum, he laid his head to one side and slept. At 3:00, after his promised hour of rest, he was still not ready. I reminded him we made a deal, although I knew his silent agreement to our deal was really just his way to get me to stop talking to him about walking. I began to take his leg compressions off, which woke him fully. He was not happy and began to tell me I didn't understand. I knew he was right; I didn't understand. But I remembered what the doctor said, and I was trying to practice my tough love on the one person

I love more than anything or anyone else on this planet. This experience was one of many times I fought between *I need to listen to Joe and how he feels* and *The doctor said to give tough love, and I have to listen to him.*

Joe finally got his legs over the side of the bed, and I knew he felt like this small feat was enough for the day. So did I, but I pushed him on. We positioned all the IVs on one side of the bed, ensuring they were untangled and looped over the pain pump that was attached to his moveable wheels. We also attached his catheter bag to the proper side of this contraption, and I made sure to have his stylish hospital gown tied just right so that we would not give anyone in the hallway a show. At that point, however, I was certain that Joe, the most modest man in America, couldn't have cared less who saw what body part of his. He was only attempting to walk so his wife would leave him alone.

He slowly pulled himself up, holding onto the steel, moveable wheels with his left hand and his seven-months-pregnant wife with his right. I had a nurse's aide helping me, following closely behind in case of a mishap. We walked—scooted, really—out of our new home away from home and rounded the corner to the left. Joe abruptly stopped as he looked at the hospital window at the end of the hall, about twenty feet away. Shrugged shoulders, slouched head, barely strong enough to look up over his brows, Joe whispered in disgust, "There is no way I can get there."

He let go of my aching shoulder and reached for his stomach in support of the wound that lay hidden beneath his shirt. I held onto his ashy, thin arms and tried to encourage him with one of my own steps, but I had to look away to wipe the tears of frustration and hurt from my cheeks. Finally, I am still not certain how, we made it down that small runway and back. Eyes bright with worry and uncertainty, my gaze never left his face.

The second we made it back to our room, Joe flopped down on the bed, hurried me to get his legs up, and was back asleep before I could get his IV cords hooked back up where they belonged and his leg compressions back on. I prayed a silent prayer, thanking God for another minute with this man.

My back was screaming from lifting, tugging, and pulling Joe down the hall. I am certain the rock-like sofa cushions and the growing baby inside of me weren't helping matters either. However, I knew after that small feat, I needed rest too. As tired as I felt, I also knew God was continuing to provide the strength I didn't have. Somehow, I said thank you, and then questioned why He could let all of this happen to us. I fell into a restless sleep.

After a short time, I was awakened by Joe's whisper, "Babe!" I waddled across the room and sat down next to him in the hospital bed. His eyes were shut, but he was trying so hard to lift his eyebrows up, evident by the crease in his forehead. I sat there, my hands rubbing his shaved head from front to back, over and over, just like I always did. And the tears began again; I thanked God again for the most perfect husband I could have ever imagined, even in my craziest dreams.

Joe smiled slightly, but then said, "Baby, something is wrong." I asked him to tell me so I could understand. He said he didn't know, but that something was definitely wrong. He just didn't feel right. I discounted his assessment, thinking whatever he was feeling was probably normal after a major surgery. I told him to rest, that the way he felt was probably because of the walk, and we would see how he felt tomorrow.

Not long after this exchange, we smelled a foul odor. We weren't sure what it was, but we were certain neither of us had ever smelled anything so awful in our lives. As nurses continued to come in to care for Joe's incision, they, too, commented on the stench that was taking over our room. Our lead nurse noticed there was drainage coming out the end of Joe's incision, right below where his belly button used to be. She told us she would let the doctor know immediately.

The next day on his rounds, the doctor noticed there was infection. He alerted us that he had instructed the nursing team to change the incision more frequently, and that he was going to remove the bottom two staples from the incision. This would allow the drainage to continue to come out and the infection to heal; the odor should also stop.

Unfortunately, it didn't. After two days of drainage and constant nagging for Joe to get up and walk, his patience was shot. This man of few words, who was more patient than anyone I'd ever encountered in my life, was ready to fight someone, hooked up to machines and all. I've never felt so sorry for him as I watched him lie with a pillow over his ghost-white face, refusing to speak to anyone. He was mortified that this repulsive smell was coming from his body and that there was nothing he could do about it.

The doctors said we would likely get to go home three to four days after surgery, but Joe continued to insist, "There is no way. I am not going home feeling like this." So, we waited for him to improve. I was exhausted but found it difficult to sleep no matter how hard I tried. Determined to nap, I pulled the hard, plastic recliner over to Joe's bedside and, for the first time, took a mild sedative to try to sleep. To this day, I don't know who contacted my OB doctor about prescribing for me this much-needed medication or who delivered it to me in the hospital. All I knew at that point was my body and mind were aching and I needed rest. As I propped myself up on a chair full of pillows and reclined my swollen legs, I grabbed Joe's hand and immediately nodded off.

After what felt like only five minutes, Joe simultaneously squeezed my hand hard, jumped up out of his bed, and screamed, "Babe, Babe, help me! Help me!" I jolted straight up out of my chair, scanning his face, as he yelled, "I am going to be sick. I am going to poop. Help me! Help me!" I grabbed a bucket and screamed to the nurse, "HELP ME! HELP ME! PLEASE HELP ME!" I held the bucket to Joe's face as a team of nurses ran into the room. We watched as the vilest, black-green liquid projected out of Joe's mouth. Right before he started vomiting, he screamed, "I have to go to the bathroom."

I remember saying, "It's okay, Baby, just go."

It all happened so fast. After it was over, a nurse asked me if I was okay as she escorted me to the couch. My response was uncontrollable dry-heaving that eventually led to getting sick myself. I could not stop crying. I was in shock and deathly afraid.

I yearned to be right there with Joe—to try to fix this, to try to bring some comfort to him. But, I also yearned not to be there because I knew he was beyond embarrassed for me to see him this way—helpless, sick, and literally pooping in his pants all at once. He was angry and frustrated. I just wanted to make it all better, but because of my own sickness and worn out body, I could not even move from the couch. I was frozen with fear, in shock, about what I had just seen.

Something was indeed wrong. We knew there were greater issues that had to be addressed sooner rather than later. I'll never forget our lead nurse's long, dark ponytail, dark eyes, and constant somber expression. She was a woman of few words, but she knew her stuff. Her movements were confident, quick, and to the point. I liked her. I knew she was going to get results. After a quick time at the nurse's station, she told us she thought there was much more infection than what the doctors had originally assumed. She informed us we would head down to get a scan done, to see what was going on in the inside. She also alerted us this would happen STAT, per doctor's orders.

As we waited for the team to come pick Joe up, I simply stared at Joe. I could not take my eyes off him. He didn't look at me, and instead stared, pissed off, at the white wall in front of him. I was ready for him to blurt out, "I give up," but inside I was begging him not to. As the team arrived to take him to the scan, Joe pleaded with his eyes for me to go with him. I willingly held his hand as they wheeled him on his hospital bed through the maze of hallways. That was a moment I will cherish forever.

The scan proved that there was, indeed, more infection where his colon was removed. Joe was completely defeated. Our surgeon informed us this was not an uncommon reaction for this part of the body after surgery. The colon is the nastiest, germiest organ, and even with a sterile operating room and equipment, infection can still develop. Our next step was to insert drain tubes into each side of Joe's abdomen, which would drain out into clear bags.

Joe began the mad cry—the cry where tears welled up in his eyes, and he tried to fight them, but they still fell down his face. Then, he got angry because he was crying, but still cried more, which made him even angrier. I hated it for him. I wanted to fix all of it. But, of course, I couldn't.

Over the next few days, nurses continued to change the drainage bags and Joe's wound. The doctor then called me to another act of tough love—to watch how the nurses did his wound care and changed the tubes and bags so I would be able to do it at home. Joe interrupted the doctor and insisted, "No!" I hushed him and told him it was fine, that I could do it.

Honestly, I wasn't sure, with my pregnancy sickness, how I would manage to keep my cookies down while I changed bags of vile, black-green liquid that smelled like rotten guts. But I knew I could do it. I had to. I watched intently and was ready to accomplish this, proving that I might make a good nurse on top of my teaching career. Joe would put a pillow over his face and hold his breath every time we changed his wound or drained his bags because he could not stand the smell. I just held my breath until it was over.

Chapter 12

Going Home

Thirteen days after we walked into Mercy Hospital, our doctor told us we could go home. He gave me a list of care instructions: to give Joe medicine at specific times, to handle his wound care and change the drain bags, and most importantly, to ensure he slept and ate. As excited as I was to go home, especially to sleep in my own bed, I was also scared I was going to do something wrong. And the thought of home left me wondering if we would be able to keep it; we had no idea what medical bills lay ahead of us or how much income we would be able to bring in to pay our existing bills. I brushed the thought away and focused on the task at hand.

I had not left the hospital once since we arrived, and I was ready to escape its nasty sterile smell that to this day makes me gag. I buzzed around our hospital home, gathering the food, drinks, gifts, and items from home that people had graciously dropped off over the previous thirteen days. Joe joked that he hadn't seen me move that fast since before I was pregnant. Our nurses had to request transportation help because of the amount of stuff we had accumulated since we moved in.

We both were ready to get back to "Paradise," the name Joe had affectionately given our home. He would always gaze out our large picture window that overlooks Table Rock Lake and say, "Everything can be going wrong, and I can look out at God's creation and know I live in paradise. That's when I know everything will work out the way it should." I hoped being home would provide us that assurance once again.

We loaded our big, white Tundra outside the revolving entrance doors at the hospital. We had just celebrated our first wedding anniversary in the hospital, and I couldn't have been more thankful. I got to celebrate my first wedding anniversary with Joe; that was all that mattered. Now, July 3, the day before our four-year dating anniversary, I somehow managed to carefully push him up into the front seat of that big truck and strap him into the front seat. He held a couch pillow up to his wounded stomach and slowly lowered his seat back. I climbed up into the driver's side of the truck and began our trek home.

This was one of only three times I remember driving while Joe was in the car. He was always the one to drive, and on the way home I was reminded why. He critiqued everything I did, every turn and every bump he felt in the road. I drove guarded, safer than I have ever driven. And yet, he could still feel every line in the road because of the pain. Although our pharmacy was on the way home, the nausea, pain and discomfort proved too much, and Joe asked me to take him straight home. I tried to convince him that I could run into the pharmacy quickly so I didn't have to make two trips, but the tears trickling down his cheeks told me what I needed to do. Again, I realized that even though I was exhausted and scared, my main priority had to be taking care of him.

Once home, I somehow got Joe up our stairs even though he could barely shuffle from one foot to the other. He leaned on me as we trudged up the stairs, my back screaming with pain under his weight. Once at the top of the stairs, we walked straight to our bedroom, and Joe sat on the edge of our bed. His abdomen was still so tender and full of pain that he could not lift his legs up onto the bed, so I did it for him. Slowly, mechanically, with rhythmic instructions, I gave him a play-by-play of what to move, when to move it, and where to move it as I guided his lower extremities to the right spots.

I watched as Joe's face turned as ghostly white as the plain white t-shirt he wore. With his eyes closed and his forehead furrowed, he pointed his chin towards the ceiling and gasped in pain. I sat down next to his feet and lay back on my back. I, too, gasped as the uncomfortable pain shot through my back and hips, yet I longed to stay in that position because I was certain that bed had never been so comfortable. Tears seeped from my eyes and fell down my face, across the tops of my ears until they hit my soft bed sheets. Joe begged with a clutch in his throat, "Babe, please go get my medicine."

In that moment, all I wanted was to keep lying there, to sleep, to never leave the four walls of our home for a very long time. And I wanted my dog. The neighbors had been keeping her fed, watered, and entertained the past thirteen days. I hadn't seen her yet; she was probably making her rounds in the neighborhood. I slowly wobbled my way back to sitting and then walked back into the summertime heat to go pick up Joe's medicine.

For the first time since I willed myself away from his pre-surgery bed, I was alone. I knew I should hurry, that Joe needed his medicine, but I found myself driving around the neighborhood yelling for my dog. I never saw her, so I finally headed toward the pharmacy. I cried the entire twenty-minute drive. I waited in the longest line I had ever seen before at this pharmacy. After speaking to the pharmacy tech, I buckled at the knees and crawled onto a bench to wait on the medicine. I watched the other customers with angry tears streaming my face. Everyone else was happy, everyone else's world did not stop, everyone else did not know what or how my life had just drastically changed. But it had. And I wanted my old life back.

Due to the high volume of traffic in our touristy town in the summer time, it took forever to fill Joe's scripts. I got a phone call from Joe while sitting on that bench, begging me to hurry. I panicked, knowing he should have taken his pain medication already and that we would be playing catch-up.

Prescriptions in hand, I waddle-ran to the truck and put the air on full blast. I ignored the urgency of eating something even though I hadn't eaten all day. As I arrived home, phone calls and texts were pouring into Joe's phone and mine—friends and family wanting to stop by to see us, to bring us whatever we needed. Though well-intentioned, these calls to help only made me exasperated. I had no energy to tell the story over again. I had no confidence that I could keep my eyes open or my back from giving out. I didn't even care that my growing son needed nourishment today. I just needed to sleep. And so did Joe.

Chapter 13

Divine Provision

A good night's rest does wonders for the body and mind. The next day was the Fourth of July, the night Joe and I shared our first date four years earlier, and he felt well enough to sit out on the porch overlooking the lake. That day, I fully recognized what surgery had done to Joe's body. He was pale, skinny, and weak. But I could not have been prouder that he was my husband and the father of our unborn son, and that I had the honor of taking care of him. I was tired—mentally, physically, emotionally—but I was happy. We were together, and this was by far the best, most meaningful anniversary I had ever had.

Joe's first hospital bill was waiting on us when we arrived home, reminding us that Joe did not have health insurance. I remember thinking, *I shouldn't even open this bill.* I knew it was the first of many, and I also knew there was no way we would ever be able to pay it in full. I did open it. It was for the very first doctor, who spent less than four minutes in our room on that first night at the hospital, to tell us he would need to send another doctor in. His bill for this expert advice? $235. I only remember this exact amount because it was the only bill I ever studied.

I still had the list of financial records the hospital needed to process our bills—to determine how much we would be required to pay. On our third day home, I gathered up the required documents and headed to the local Social Services Office, the very office I had worked in only two years prior. My former co-workers were now the ones who would help me. Dropping off the bank statements, tax returns, bills paid, copies of identification, and other personal documents proved to be one of the most humbling experiences of my life. I stood in line amongst those who also needed assistance, those who could not afford to meet their basic needs, whether it be food, shelter, daycare, or health insurance. My pride and ego took the greatest hit they had ever taken, but I stood there, allowing the tears to streak my face. I loved my husband more than my desire to reject the help we so desperately needed.

Less than two weeks later, I received a phone call from the Social Services Office stating they needed another piece of documentation and they wanted to do an in-person interview. I sat down with a former co-worker, who cared more about my personal well-being than what we were about to discuss. At this point, I was just grateful she cared. After discussing the lesson we had learned about not having health insurance for Joe, she told me there would be a review of documentation and that they would call me soon with the decision.

The next morning, my phone rang before 9:00 a.m., just as I had fallen into a restful sleep after a restless night. I stepped outside on my front porch, leaving my husband sleeping peacefully, and sat down on my white porch swing. Thank goodness for the support of that swing when the Social Services office told me the decision: the state's Medicaid would retroactively take care of Joe's medical bills for only a small out-of-pocket expense. Everything would be taken care of. Unbeknownst to us, the doctor had already declared Joe permanently disabled; this status is why Medicaid would cover his expenses. They informed me I should apply for Social Security Disability benefits for Joe, but we would have to wait six months before he would receive the benefits. I bawled. I was speechless; yet again, God was taking care of us in miraculous ways.

I had been convinced that all those days in the hospital would cost us our home and all our belongings. Those medical bills totaled more than I would make in a lifetime. How could we ever pay them? I had already put a price-tag on anything I thought we could sell out of our home. Joe hadn't seemed to worry about this like I did; he always seemed to know it would work out.

One evening while he was still in the hospital, he woke up momentarily from his sedated state and caught me crying. When asked what I was crying about, I told him I was terrified that we were going to lose everything. His response, with eyes half open, was, "We have lots of friends, Babe. We will be fine." Then, he dozed back off. I was angry at him because he wasn't worrying about this very real problem. But he knew. And in that moment on the porch swing, I realized I needed to learn more lessons from my husband about faith.

Before I could wipe the tears from my face and regain enough strength to walk in to tell Joe the great news, my phone rang again. It was a humid morning, and the gray Mizzou t-shirt I had on was already showing the outline of my perspiring pregnant belly. It was my best friend, Nikki. I assumed she was just calling to check on us, but she wasn't. She called to relay the news that the Herschend family, a well-known family in our area, had decided to pay our electric bill for the next three months. Though many know this family for their theme parks and other attractions, most don't know their hearts to serve their community.

As a teacher, I had gotten a glimpse of their generosity in providing support for underprivileged students in our community and many other surrounding communities. Their family's organization provides funds to the area schools so that they can help assist kids with a variety of needs, such as the costs associated with extra-curricular activities, school supplies, clothing, and many other needs. To know that their family also seeks out families in need and provides support was unbelievable. They continued to prove their love and grace for our family throughout our entire story.

Friends, acquaintances, neighbors, and even strangers brought money, called to pay our bills, and stopped at nothing to recruit others to help us get through financially. They set up a benefit fundraiser and a Facebook page to keep everyone informed of our latest needs. Their love never stopped. Throughout our journey, we never missed a payment. We were never cold or without food. This is unfathomable to me. We had a huge mortgage payment and massive credit card debt on top of all our regular expenses. Joe couldn't work, and I would be off work for six weeks of maternity leave. Yet, we were completely taken care of. This was God at work in the hearts of His people.

In addition to the financial support, we spent much of the next month visiting with long-lost friends and family who stopped by to bring more food than we could eat and other things we needed. Hugs were shared, prayers were given, and tears were shed. Love came in and out, every day, all day long. Despite the chaos of life that made it difficult for us to be consistent with our friends and family, their love never disappeared.

Chapter 14

Slowing Down

One evening a few weeks later, Joe was quite tired, which was his new normal. After getting him into bed, I checked back in on him and noticed his cheeks glowed red and his face was hot to my touch. It was less than a month since his total colectomy, and he still had drainage coming from the end of his wound. Instinctively, I knew something was wrong.

I immediately called the nurse's line. They informed me I needed to get him to the emergency room immediately, that a fever meant infection. Joe refused to go. I paced back and forth in our bedroom, fearful and doubting Joe's decision to stay home that night. I certainly did not want to go either, but I wanted to know he was going to be okay. He promised if the fever was not gone by the morning, he would let me take him to the doctor. This type of banter between us would recur many times during our cancer journey. He hated being in the hospital and always put up a fight. But as destiny would have it, in me he met his hard-headed match. Somehow, I always got him to the hospital when he needed to be there.

This time was no different. We went to the hospital. Our surgeon confirmed that Joe's infection was on the inside. Although Joe's abdominal incision was healing on the outside, the tissue was not fusing together underneath. Essentially, the tissue was rotting, hence the smell and the drainage. The surgeon informed us Joe would have to have another surgery that would enable the wound to heal from the inside out. As the doctor turned around to leave the room, Joe lay still on his back on the exam table. I stood up, looked at him, and watched as tears trickled from his closed eyes down into his ears.

Like many moments, I didn't know what to say, and I began to cry too. I leaned down to kiss his forehead and whispered, "It will be okay," but he pushed me away. I never felt rejected, per se, when Joe did this. He did it a lot. My comforting him always made him cry more. He would always say something like, "Don't, I don't want to cry." I never did understand why he didn't want to cry in front of me. Then again, I'm not sure why I didn't want to cry in front of him either.

We scheduled another surgery for the end of July. Joe dreaded it much worse than me, but he, of course, was the one who had to deal with the physical repercussions. Though he never told me directly, I think he was worried I would not find him attractive because of his scars. He offered enough off-the-cuff "jokes" about the topic that, in hindsight, I realize he was actually concerned.

Surgery morning arrived. We had to be at the hospital at 6:00 a.m., an hour away from our home. The surgery did not last long, and, thankfully, I wasn't as scared as I was before his first one. I still paced, though. I still worried, and I still begged God to let this surgery fix everything. Dr. B came out to tell me the surgery went well. He informed me he would not even consider letting Joe stay in the hospital overnight, that he was fine to go home. He also explained I would have to dress his wound—a rather large, gaping hole in his stomach—two to three times a day. Though I had a list of questions about this, I told him I was sure I could do it. I had to do it. As much as I wanted someone else to do the hard things during our journey, it had to be me. However, I had to attend a new teacher meeting the next day, and I wanted to make sure it would be okay if I left him home by himself. The doctor confirmed it would be, then proceeded to ask me something that caught me off guard.

Dr. B, for the first time in the many encounters we had in the past month, didn't seem hurried or rushed. As if we were accustomed to casual conversation, he asked, "What do you and Joe do for your careers?"

Surprised, I wearily responded, "I am a special education teacher and coach girls' basketball. Joe runs our small business as a mechanic."

To this day, his response makes me ponder. The most genuine smile spread across his face, and he said, "You guys are great, really great." Even more in shock, I smiled too. We shook hands and confirmed we would make a follow up appointment. Knowing now that Dr. B didn't just see Joe and I as patients, but as people with a real life and a real story, gave me the bounce in my step I desperately needed.

Joe came out groggy, as usual, from surgery. Once he was more awake, I told him we would be going home that day and that I would have to do the wound changes. His eyes revealed his concern. I told him I would be fine, that there was no need to worry. He always did, though. Through all his surgeries and sickness, he was always more worried about me and how I would handle it all—yet another reason I love this man so much. He always put me first, even in his times of greatest need.

Like our last car ride home after surgery, Joe felt every bump in the road, every line in the pavement. I tried my best to drive in a way that would keep him comfortable, but he let me know I was failing at that task every time he winced and cried out in pain. I was agitated and frustrated. This moment felt like so many others would during Joe's illness. Despite trying so hard to be everything he needed, I felt like I constantly failed.

We finally made it home. The next morning, after eating and taking his medication, Joe was ready to try to take a shower. He leaned on me and hobbled his way to the bathroom, holding his stomach. Joe could not bend over to get his clothes off, so I carefully undressed him. He requested to keep the bandage and packing in his wound so he could take it out in the shower by himself. Though concerned, I agreed. Honestly, I was ready for a few minutes of rest without Joe needing me. I had not been sitting for more than three minutes when Joe began screaming. Rushing out of my oasis of the black recliner, I ran to the bathroom.

"What? What? What's wrong?" I continued to repeat. His back was to me in the shower, and I couldn't get him to look at me.

Scanning frantically for an answer I could see, I only heard him cry out: "Babe, you can't do this. We can't do this. You can't do this. We can't do this, Babe. You can't. We can't." Over and over and over, he repeated those words.

Assuming he was talking about his large wound that he was seeing for the first time, I assured him we could. I opened the shower door and shut the water off. Joe looked over his shoulder at me, revealing his white, ghastly face and his tears. My heart ached as he slowly turned around and displayed an image I could have never imagined. Knowing that he was anticipating my reaction, I remember telling myself, *Do not over react. Do not show a facial expression. Just tell him it will be okay.*

The wound was shocking, though, and I am not quite sure if I hid the shock well or not. It scared me. I had never seen anything like it. The wound opened from between the bottom of his rib cage to his waist line. He didn't have a belly button anymore; it had been cut through. I felt my eyes get wide, and then I could see him looking at me. I also noticed he was trembling and getting weak.

I wrapped him in a towel, much like a young boy, and he closed his eyes and whispered as he fell into me, "Babe, I can't walk. I think I am going to be sick."

"Okay, okay. It's okay; we will get this," I remember assuring him. But I'm not actually sure how I managed. I steadied Joe on the bathroom counter, trying to balance myself, to protect my baby belly, and to keep Joe upright. Somehow, we managed to get twisted around, and I put Joe on my back. I slowly walked him back into our bedroom, balancing him enough that I could turn back around and set him on the edge of the bed. Joe began to weep, and as he did, I repeated over and over, "It's okay, Baby. We will get through this. It is okay. It is not that bad. I can take care of the wound. It will be fine."

He never responded. He only sat there with pissed-off tears slowly streaking his face. Avoiding the uncomfortable silence, I continued to ramble about who knows what. I dried his weak, thin body off with a towel and talked him through what I was doing as I put on his clothes. The incision through Joe's abdominal muscles limited his ability to even lift his legs up onto the bed, let alone bend over to put on his underwear and shorts. Step-by-step, I half-assured him and half-assured myself what we were doing as we were doing it: "Okay, I am lifting your right foot up just a little bit to get your underwear on."

I glanced over my brow to see his face wincing in pain. The tears were still streaking his cheeks as he closed his eyes and lifted his face toward the ceiling. That inevitable lump was there, yet again, in my throat. I could not begin to imagine how awkward, uncomfortable, and humiliating it was for Joe to have his eight-months-pregnant wife dress him, yet I had never been so honored to be the one to extend this act of love.

"Okay, Baby, now I am going to lift your left leg up just a little bit and put it through the leg hole." As I slipped his foot through, I noticed his face was still in that upward position, fists balled up on the bed next to him. Then came the hardest part. "Okay, Baby, now I am going to have to lift you up slowly and pull your shorts and underwear up at the same time. You can just lean into me on my shoulders as I do this."

At that point, I heard a muffled gasp of pain and felt his death grip on my shoulders, making obvious his unstable stance. I braced myself to ensure we both didn't go down as I gently pulled his clothing up to his waist. His incision ran so low, I had to leave his pants unbuttoned. I slowly lowered his bony body back onto the edge of the bed and realized he needed to catch his breath. On the count of three, I lifted his legs up and got him settled in bed.

Those next few weeks, we did a lot of resting—our new normal. We didn't leave the house except to refill medication and for doctors' appointments. While at home, we didn't do any work, preferring to rest in the comfort of our own bed, and each other. Though I would not have chosen it, I am grateful that Joe's sickness required us to slow down. Although I hate to admit it, I realize that nothing else could have forced us to slow down our lives more. I am eternally grateful for that gift.

Chapter 15

Unexpected

In August, we had our first doctor's appointment with the oncologist to discuss Joe's options for chemotherapy. After initial blood work, the doctor requested we do one more CT scan to make sure the cancer was still contained to Joe's colon before he started chemotherapy treatments. He had the CT scan, and we waited for the results.

That same week, I spent time in my classroom to prepare for the new school year. Exhausted and consumed with worry for Joe, my heart simply was not in it. My nine-month swollen belly didn't seem to help matters either. I did the bare minimum. I was also required to attend back-to-school meetings with other new teachers to the district. Since I was new, I assumed many would not be aware of my complicated situation—both expecting and my husband being diagnosed with cancer. I was wrong. Word had traveled fast, and I was welcomed by these new colleagues with kind gestures and offers to help us during this most difficult time.

After one of these new-teacher meetings, Joe and I attended a benefit fundraiser set up by one of Joe's friends. The outpouring of love from our small-town community, and from our friends and family, was the greatest blessing of all during our journey of fighting cancer. This event, held at a local pub, was an outpouring of love. The pub was filled to capacity, with standing room only. As we looked around the room, we were in awe of how many people loved us and wanted to support us.

Joe had friends he had not seen since high school who were there, ready and willing to take whatever burden we could pass onto them. I had friends who had driven over an hour to show their love and support. They had a silent auction and collected donations from the many who were willing to give.

These people, our army, were going to be there to get us through. It was simply incredible. My heart was full; God had given us such a gift in Joe. I wondered how, out of all these people in this crowded restaurant, I was the luckiest of all to be Joe's wife and best friend.

The day before the first day of school, our district hosted an evening open house for students and their parents to meet their new teachers for the year. That morning, we received the results of the CT scan. The cancer had already spread to Joe's liver, and he had blood clots on his lungs; he would need to start chemo immediately. We were devastated. My school administrators insisted that I stay home with Joe instead of coming to the open house and that they would take care of sharing my information with my students and their parents. Though I appreciated their offer, I came to open house. During this event, I was able to warn parents of my impending arrival, as well as that my husband was sick. I forewarned them of the possibility of excessive absences but assured them their students would be in good hands.

The first day of school went smoothly, except for my excessive pain. I had been uncomfortable; however, as the day progressed, the pain was nearly unmanageable. I was not able to sit, stand, or get in any comfortable position. When the last bell rang and students were taken to the buses, I felt a warmness spread from my face to my toes. I knew I needed to go home to get Joe and then get to the hospital, but I was panicked. I wasn't sure if I could even drive home. And even if I could, I didn't know if Joe could drive us to the hospital with his fanny pack that was infusing him with powerful chemotherapy.

Calmly gathering my things, I somehow walked toward my car, my eyes focused on my feet and an inner voice that was whispering, "Get home, just get home. Go get Joe." I remember someone asking me if I was okay as I passed through my school's brightly lit commons area, and I vaguely remember saying no. Once I got into our truck, I saw a team of teachers running toward me and then crowding outside my driver's door. Many teachers and our principal begged me to let them take me to the hospital. The pleas and demands were numerous, but my answer stayed the same, "I am not going to that hospital without Joe." All I knew was I was the one who had the truck, and so Joe had no way of meeting me at the hospital. I was not about to deliver our son by myself.

Finally, a plan was made for a teacher to follow me home in her car. While I watched her in my rear-view mirror, I waited for Joe's voice on the other end of the phone. Immediately, he knew something was wrong. After giving him the run-down of my pain, and the fact that I could hardly breathe, I asked if he was sick from the chemo. He denied he was, but the faltering in his voice told me otherwise. I asked him to get our bags and be ready to go when I got home. As I pulled into our driveway, there he stood, with our bags at the bottom of our deck stairs. The teacher who had followed me home got me upstairs and changed my clothes as if I were a little girl. Yelling for someone to grab the camera, Joe escorted me outside to the truck.

Less than a mile up the road, Joe's dad met us and parked his truck in a neighbor's yard. He took over the driver's seat, and Joe tried to soothe me during the hour-long drive to the hospital. The drive was painful and scary, and I screamed from the contractions. That tiny baby seemed ready, even though his dad and I were not.

Despite the contractions, the doctor determined the baby was, in fact, not ready to make his appearance. They sent us home to rest, hoping I could wait another week before delivering. Rest is exactly what we did as we anticipated seeing our son for the first time.

Chapter 16

Our Miracle is Delivered

Porter Boycen Smith arrived six days later on August 21, 2013. Though it was difficult for my body, the delivery was also difficult for Joe's body. Only three days prior, Joe had completed seventy-two hours of chemo, so he was exhausted. He was also physically ill. Though I didn't realize it while in labor, Joe made countless trips to the bathroom to get sick, but he always returned to my side.

Finally, after sixteen and a half hours of labor, Porter was ready to make his entrance. Our son's sweet daddy beamed with pride as the doctor instructed us both to reach down and pull our son into our arms after he was delivered. In that moment, when the three of us became one, I saw true love re-birthed in my husband's crystal blue eyes.

The appreciation, unconditional love, and admiration he had for me in that moment was priceless and left me speechless. As we snuggled together in those moments after Porter's birth, I felt complete, like I had all I would ever need in this lifetime. My husband held our son, his tiny hand wrapped around his sleeping daddy's finger. This image is forever etched in my mind—the first of many hospital campouts as a family of three.

As we settled in for the night, we examined every inch of our new baby boy. His fingernail beds were square just like his daddy's, taking my breath away. The shape of his forehead, the widow's peak, his high-arched eyebrows, and his blue, blue eyes—it was like looking at a tiny version of Joe's face. Though I was still hopeful God would miraculously heal my husband, I realized in that moment that Porter was the miracle we had prayed for, the miracle we desperately needed as we continued this journey. He brought joy, healing, and hope that nothing else could.

Chapter 17

Returning to Regular Life

We settled into life at home. Less than one week after our son's arrival, Joe's oncologist decided it was necessary to try a different type of chemotherapy regimen. Patients in the Midwest were required to have their first dosage of this new chemotherapy administered in the hospital, under careful observation of medical staff, because of the environmental reactions that had been reported in the region. The three of us made our way to the hospital for what would become a common refrain—Joe at the hospital for treatment, fighting for his life, while cuddling his brand-new baby.

Only four weeks after Porter's birth, I was to be the maid-of honor in my childhood best friend's wedding. Although completely elated for her, I couldn't help but have a tinge of jealousy in my heart. I was jealous that her life seemed perfect and jealous that life was moving forward for everyone else while our life seemed to be crumbling. Yes, Joe and I were married and had our first child, beautiful blessings, but I felt we shouldn't have had to fight cancer, not at this stage of life. Yet here we were. Life was moving on, and we were determined to roll with it as best as we could. Joe, despite being in severe pain, accompanied Porter and me to the wedding.

After six weeks of maternity leave, with dread, I headed back to work. I knew I would struggle with leaving my baby, but it made it even worse to also have to leave Joe. Whenever I thought about it, I felt as though I could not breathe. The days felt even longer than I thought they would. During recesses and lunch period, I would jog across the parking lot to our district's daycare and nurse our sweet baby, thankful to get to see him, but always yearning for more time with him. To complicate matters further, basketball season was quickly approaching, which extended my days by two and a half hours. During my junior high girls' basketball practices, I would coach with my eight-week-old baby on my hip, doing my best to get my team ready for the season.

Joe's oncology appointments were on Thursdays, every other week, and he would have eight-hour long infusions of chemotherapy. Because I was working, I had to schedule someone each week to take Joe to and from his appointments. Though I could usually find help with transportation, what I could not ensure was that information about his medications, pain levels, and symptoms were being communicated appropriately to the doctors and nurses. Therefore, I began to take off work on these Thursdays to be present at the doctor appointments.

After his eight-hour infusions, Joe was hooked up to a fanny pack full of chemotherapy that continuously infused him until Saturday afternoon. The treatments always left him violently ill and physically exhausted. He was either puking or sleeping. Joe's pain never left him, and he suffered severe side effects from the chemo, such as loss of appetite, rapid weight loss, excessive diarrhea, mouth sores, and depression. Taking care of Joe physically, including managing his medication, and caring for Porter left little time to do anything outside our four walls. Watching my husband suffer, unable to ease his discomfort, was devastating. However, I cherished this time at home. Even though it was hectic and often difficult, we were together, which was all I wanted.

Chapter 18

Complications

Joe's pain never completely went away. Before his pain in one area would resolve, he would experience pain in another. The battle to find the right dosage of medication to ease his pain was ongoing. Joe consistently complained about a painful area on his "butt-bone" that made it nearly impossible for him to sit. After trying to ease the pain with heating pads, hot baths, and his daily dosage of pain medications, and with no clear answers from our oncologist, we finally went back to our original surgeon who diagnosed Joe with an anal fistula. Because Joe no longer had his colon, anything he ate or drank would go straight through him. This plus chemotherapy increased the number of times he needed to use the bathroom to between nine and twelve times per day.

Eventually, Joe developed a bowel obstruction. Because he was in so much pain from the anal fistula, he was unable to go to the bathroom, eventually causing the blockage. He started throwing up, so I made an appointment with the oncologist that his dad took him to while I was at work. Highly concerned, Joe's oncologist office called me to tell me Joe had walked out of his appointment, yet he appeared very ill and in grave pain.

Furiously mad, I ran into my principal's office, yelling about my departure and letting her know I would be in contact soon. Battling a screaming two-month-old and Joe, angry at cancer, I was beside myself. I found him in his shop, where he had created a livelihood for our family, yet could not anymore. He was throwing tools, parts, and equipment, and I stood in horror, not knowing what to do. I wanted to fix it all—the pain, the cancer—but I could think of nothing to say. I was angry at him for walking out of his doctor's appointment, even while he was still throwing up, and for the months of his pushing back against the doctors' suggestions. I needed him to be willing to go to the doctor's office so we could figure this out. But instead, he was angry in a place he used to be on top of his game.

Finally, I convinced him to get in the car, though he yelled at me to get him down to the house. Although I tried to talk to him, ask questions, and get conversation going so I would know what to do, Joe stormed off into our room, ignoring every word I said. This was not like my husband. He never ignored me or my feelings, and he never raised his voice at me. And yet here I was taking all his anger, unable to fix any of it.

Joe proceeded to get sick again and demanded to be left alone. Joe's friend, Jon, showed up and easily convinced him to go to the doctor with me. Once there, the doctor decided that we, indeed, needed to be admitted to the hospital. As I was driving a sick husband and a tired baby to the hospital, I placed a few phone calls to friends who grabbed our essentials from home for our stay.

Once at the hospital, it occurred to me that our son would be spending his first Halloween there. In that moment, the reality of my life felt the furthest from what I could have hoped for. I was sad, depressed, and angry that our family didn't get to be like normal families, who would soon be celebrating their cute little babies dressed up as sweet little pumpkins. Instead, we were getting all the frights and scares of being in a hospital room.

Later that evening, as the lights began to turn out, Porter and I got comfortable in a reclining chair. Hospital pillows stuffed on my sides and behind my back, we snuggled in for the night. Because we were sharing a room with an elderly couple and only had the privacy of a paper sheet in between our temporary living spaces, I was keenly aware of keeping Porter quiet through the night. I had already scouted out my trail to the visitors' waiting area where I would go when he woke up to nurse in the middle of the night.

Two nurses approached the room and quizzically looked at Porter's and my make-shift bed. One nurse proceeded to ask if I had planned to stay the night. Upon confirming I did, she looked at the other nurse standing in the doorway, concerned. After a few awkward moments, she responded with, "I don't know if that is the best idea."

Without giving her time to express her concerns, I responded with, "I don't know if it is the best idea either, but when you have a newborn baby and sick husband, please let me know what you would do."

Both nurses walked out without further communication. That night, I got little sleep, but my sweet husband was finally resting peacefully. That night, October 31, 2013, I got to witness my two gifts—Porter and Joe—sleep peacefully. This was the moment that I had all I ever needed, all in the same room as me. I had never been so in love. Nothing else could have made my life feel more complete. It wasn't ideal. I wished we weren't here at all. But I had them—my people, my family—all together, in one room, loving each other. That was pure happiness.

Chapter 19

Our First and Only Holidays

The concerns I had on June 22, 2013, that my husband would not be alive for our first holidays diminished as we approached Thanksgiving. Joe's blood work had come back that his cancer markers were at an astonishing four! They had been over two hundred, and the doctor and nurses could not believe he was responding so well. The chemo was working!

I jumped out of the car and ran into his arms to tell him the news. I choked up, and I thanked him for going through the hell of chemotherapy. He smiled genuinely for the first time since our son was born, and I felt hope in this journey again. I felt like he knew it was all worth it, and that he had new commitment to keep up with the chemo, despite the sickness, exhaustion, and now the facial breakout that covered his face.

Thanksgiving gave us a five-day weekend together. We looked forward to traveling to see family, no chemotherapy, and time together. What we didn't account for was that Joe would continue to be sick. So much so that at his cousin's house, Joe would not get out of bed unless he was running to the bathroom to throw up. I felt lonely without him present in our conversations with family, and I struggled with feeling like I was abandoning him while he was downstairs sick.

Joe's taste buds were completely out of whack. Chemotherapy made everything taste like a ball of wax. To his disappointment, he still didn't have much of an appetite, so he didn't eat much. After a couple of days, we traveled to his aunt and uncle's house in St. Louis, where he was less sick. Here, Joe was able to eat a little more, which seemed to improve his mood.

On our way home from St. Louis, Joe finally made his first joke about his diagnosis. He looked at me in the rearview mirror with his smirky grin and said, "I think it's weird to say I have cancer of the butt, but I guess I do." He started laughing. I nervously looked up at him and then began dying laughing.

Joe proceeded to declare that that was what he was going to start telling people. He also informed me we needed to create an atlas of the best bathrooms around the country. Confused, yet humored, I played along with this idea. He informed me, "Babe, just think about it. We all hate when we pull into a gas station to use the bathroom, and they are disgusting and have the worst toilet paper in there."

Shaking my head, I wasn't sure what to think about this declaration and newfound humor about his situation. Joe was as quiet as I am outgoing, even in private moments with me. He sure hadn't laughed about any of this cancer stuff yet, but this day proved different. Excited that we could joke and not just cry anymore, I enjoyed our humor and our exciting bathroom-promotion venture!

At Christmas, Joe didn't feel much better and still didn't have much of an appetite. The chemo made his taste buds react in two different ways, neither helping his appetite. Sometimes, Joe fought the "ball of wax" taste. No matter how salty, sweet, or flavorful something was, he could only taste wax. Other times, however, whatever he ate tasted like someone dumped an entire shaker of salt on it. He was humiliated and frustrated, and he continued to be discouraged.

On top of the eating issues, Joe became extremely cold no matter where we were. He would often sleep downstairs on the couch right next to our fire place. On Christmas morning, Joe had our house at eighty degrees. Although the rest of us were about to melt, he continued to be cold. I cannot understand how chemotherapy can have so many adverse effects on one's body, all at once.

That Christmas, so many angels blessed our family. Underneath our Christmas tree were gifts from our oncologist's office, as well as friends, family, and strangers in our community. Many times during our journey with cancer, love really did shine brighter than our misfortunes. Our family was together on Christmas morning, next to our warm fireplace and the blessings of so many. It was the perfect Christmas. It would be the only Christmas all together.

Chapter 20

Setbacks

Our winter break at school got extended by Mother Nature. We had more snow days that winter than I ever remember having, even when I was a kid. The only unfortunate part of snow days is trying to navigate our steep driveway, which becomes a sheet of ice when bad weather comes. Four-wheel drive doesn't even help us get out of the driveway. Lucky for us, we only needed to be home, as Joe was recovering from his round of chemotherapy. I think those snow days were God's gift to us, His way of slowing down everyday life. We could see the beautiful scene outside, but we were "stuck" inside to enjoy those we loved the most.

On one of these snowy days, I was home with Porter, who had RSV. I had to give him breathing treatments, which he loathed. Every time, I had to physically restrain him to complete the treatment. Meanwhile, Joe barely moved from the recliner in our bedroom, heating pad on his back, as the television moved from one channel to another. In those moments, I thought to myself, *If something happens to Joe, what would I do to get someone down here to help me?* Then, like a self-fulfilling prophecy, I heard a loud THUMP in the master bathroom. My heart felt like it stopped beating for a moment, and then raced to uncontrollable speeds.

Quickly, I jumped up, turned the breathing machine off, and laid down a screaming, infuriated four-month-old in the middle of the bedroom floor. I ran the few steps to the bathroom and saw my husband on his back, convulsing in the middle of the floor. Panicked, all I heard myself saying was "Babe, Babe, BABE. Don't do this to me. Don't you dare do this to me."

The baby was still screaming; Joe was looking at me through his glasses, sheer panic in his eyes. He didn't stop convulsing. I pleaded and screamed, "Babe!" over and over and begged him not to die. I knew I should call someone for help, but I also wanted to stay by his side and get him to come to. All the while, my baby, still in the middle of the bedroom floor, was screaming. He needed me too. I froze, hunched over his body, staring into his eyes that were begging me to help and at his mouth that couldn't speak.

Suddenly, his body released his muscles, and he lay his head on the floor. I grabbed my phone to call 911. Joe began talking and said, "I am okay." Knowing what I had just seen, I knew he was not okay. I heard our son, still crying, as I screamed into my phone, asking for someone to come and help me. From the bathroom floor, Joe begged me to hang up and tried to convince me he was okay. I walked away from the bedroom, from the two people I love the most, and was finally able to give the operator the information she needed to send help.

Once the paramedics arrived, I had stopped screaming. However, it was replaced with uncontrollable crying. Porter was looking at me like I had lost my mind. Joe was angry—angry that it had happened, angry that I had called for help. The paramedics told us Joe was severely dehydrated and lacked the proper nutrients in his body. This made sense; Joe hadn't eaten in days. The paramedics said it was up to me whether they take him to the hospital. Knowing Joe was already angry with me for calling, I called off the troops and told them we would follow up with our doctor. I watched as the paramedics left our house and climbed down our slick, icy driveway on foot toward the ambulance parked on the street. We weren't going anywhere that night.

Joe was rather quiet the rest of the evening; he was weak. His body was fighting infection, cancer, chemotherapy, and, we found out at our doctor's appointment the next day, the flu. He couldn't bring himself to put anything in his stomach, and he couldn't have kept it there if he tried. The doctor pumped him with fluids, double what they thought it would take, and he was finally in a bit better shape.

It was never just the fight against cancer that was difficult; it was all the other struggles that came along with it, and that winter there were many. But I was so thankful for my time at home with Porter and Joe that snowy and icy winter, even with the added struggles. It would be our last winter together.

Chapter 21

The Real Bad News Begins

In March, Porter celebrated his seven-month birthday, and we couldn't have been prouder parents. He was complete and pure joy. He was a happy child, always content, and no matter what we were doing, he rolled with it. Whether we were in hospital rooms, doctors' offices, or at home doing nothing, Porter was content to be with us. Every day I was, and am, thankful for his sweet, calm spirit that is just like his dad's. To this day, he carries this gift with him.

Spring had begun, and we were still on our regimen of three days of chemotherapy, every other week. Joe was tolerating it, but he was on different mixtures than when he first began. We spent most of our time at home, Joe too sick or too tired to do much of anything. Occasionally, we were able to go out, drive around town, and maybe even grab a hamburger. However, most trips involved a sudden change of direction right back home because Joe was nauseated or just too tired.

One Friday evening—the weather was perfect—we celebrated Joe's birthday. No special hoopla, just together—Joe on the bench, Porter and I playing on the porch with toys dragged out from inside the house. My phone rang, a hospital number calling. I knew something wasn't right; it was late on a Friday night. I shifted Porter to Joe who was sitting on the porch swing. There, on our refinished porch swing, sat two people who loved each other in a way I still cannot describe. Porter, in his sweet caterpillar pajamas, fell asleep in his daddy's arms as Joe rocked him back and forth.

Though I didn't want to look away from this sweet scene, I moved to the back porch to answer the call. I wanted to be able to talk, and listen, without anyone else hearing, specifically Joe. I found myself doing this quite often. I wanted to know the information first, and process it, before I had to tell Joe. It was our oncologist calling. Joe's scans came back and were not showing improvement; in fact, they were showing growth. There was also a lymph node just outside the liver that was suspicious. There was nothing more they could do. We had changed chemo regimens multiple times in nine months. Our options, except for a clinical trial, were exhausted. Choking back tears, pacing back and forth, and looking out at the serene lake, I wondered what we were going to do. How could this really be happening?

I had prayed to my God. I had boldly told him what I wanted; He was supposed to answer boldly. My faith was one hundred percent in Him. I had never been closer to Him. I had never trusted Him more, yet this was happening. How was I supposed to go back through the house to the front porch to tell Joe we would need to get another opinion, somewhere else? How do I tell him we are closer to the end, an end we haven't talked about, that we haven't even considered a possibility? Because it wasn't. He wasn't going to die. And we were going to find a way.

I walked into the house and went straight to the bathroom. Tears flooded my cheeks. Short, small gasps of air I was trying to suck in would escape and cause the faintest of noises. I didn't want him to see me cry. I didn't want him to think I believed the fate that lay ahead. I needed to be strong. I just couldn't pull it together. I had no one I could call—he would hear me. I couldn't leave—they both needed me.

To the shower I went. My oasis. The place I went every single time I needed three minutes to be by myself. The drum of the showering water would drown out my cries to God to bring the miracle we needed. I stood in there and sobbed. I sobbed, leaning into my shower wall, and then on my hands and knees, until I was able to walk out. My face was red, like the rest of my scorched body. I tried to tell myself that my husband would never know I had just been crying.

Once I walked backed out onto the porch, I was ready to fight for Joe's life. I told Joe I thought we should go for another opinion somewhere else and that I would call several places on Monday. I couldn't bring myself to reveal any other details of the call, but I'm sure Joe could figure out what was going on. Calm and steady, Joe shook his head and walked back into the house with Porter in his arms. Joe lay Porter in our bed and then crawled into bed with him, and they both fell asleep.

The weekend gave me time to research. Monday gave me the news I didn't want to hear—since Joe now had Medicaid, our bills would be covered only if we went to a hospital in Missouri. MD Anderson was out. Mayo Clinic was out. However, the next week after a routine visit to our oncologist, he put in a request for treatment at Siteman Cancer Center in St. Louis, Missouri.

Due to the urgency of our situation, Joe's visit got pushed up. In less than a month, we were sitting in front of three different doctors, with three different options: 1) a surgically implanted pump that would continuously infuse chemotherapy to his liver, 2) a clinical trial, and 3) a different type of chemotherapy that would require us to stay in St. Louis all summer. After hearing all the options, Joe told me, "It's up to you." Although I appreciated, and still do, his confidence and trust in my decisions, I didn't want this burden on me. I did not want to choose the wrong option. I did not want all the weight of this decision to fall on my shoulders. I wanted him to tell me what he wanted. I just wanted something, anything, to be easy. I needed it to be. But it wasn't going to be. It was only going to get harder.

Eventually, Joe expressed his opinions about the treatment options. After his horrendous experiences with recovering from surgery already on this journey, he took that option off the table. He also refused the option of summer-long chemo in St. Louis. That left the clinical trial, only available through Siteman. With this option, we would travel back and forth to St. Louis every other week. We were hopeful that this would work. After all, God does work in mysterious ways, right?

We completed the paperwork for the trial and waited to hear that Joe was randomly chosen to be in the group that would receive the trial chemotherapy regimen. Except he wasn't. Joe had been placed in the group who would receive chemo we knew didn't work. We were out. We chose to come home to process the news and to decide how to move forward. Our road trip home initiated a season of pain of both soul and body that was often too much to bear.

With all three options out, we decided we would try additional types of chemotherapy, mostly in an effort to manage Joe's pain, which was horrendous. Despite my frantic pacing and unwavering efforts to figure out how to make Joe comfortable, his pain only intensified. I could not help him. We decided to seek help from Springfield, Missouri's most expensive hotel—Mercy Hospital.

Chapter 22

Pain

My husband. Well, my favorite word to describe him is "mine." A few other ways I love to describe him are kind, sweet, tender-hearted, compassionate, hardworking, determined, creative, innovative, and immensely talented. Another few words are stubborn, bull-headed, and strong-willed. During Joe's fight, we needed him to be all those things, and I really did love these characteristics in him until, of course, they worked against me. Joe's stubbornness, bull-headedness, and strong-will made each of our trips to Mercy Hospital in Springfield that summer difficult, to say the least.

Pain enveloped every inch of Joe's body. Every night, in between nursing Porter seven to nine times, I would awaken to Joe's screams. His pain was unbearable, and he begged me to do something to help. Desperate to ease his suffering, I often resorted to giving him his high dosage pain medication sooner than I was supposed to, but even this did not touch his pain. There was simply nothing else I could do at home. We needed help to get his pain manageable, but Joe fought me every time we needed to go to the hospital, and often he refused to go.

I'm really not certain why Joe exerted his stubbornness, bull-headedness, and strong-will over going to the hospital other than he just didn't want to be there. I mean, who wants to be in the hospital? Certainly, it wasn't ideal for our family to spend days, sometimes weeks, there. But he did get relief from his pain. So, I made it my priority to get him there, even though I knew he would fight me.

Not too far into the summer, I figured out how to get him to the hospital and to avoid conflict. Whenever Joe's pain reached unbearable levels, I just "made an appointment" with our oncologist because I knew we would be told to go immediately to the hospital to be admitted. Joe attempted to fight in the middle of the doctor's office, but at least I had backup. And at least we were right next door, not an hour away in the comfort of our home. Prior to each appointment, I secretly set out clothes for him, myself, and Porter. A phone call or text to my loyal friend I taught with meant she would go pick up the clothes, as well as the pillows, toys, and snacks I would need to survive the next week, or weeks, at the hospital with my husband and our sweet nine-month old baby.

We spent many weeks that summer living in a hospital room. Porter learned to crawl in a hospital room. He pretended to use a phone for the first time in his daddy's hospital bed. We captured sweet baby giggles and daddy-son chats on video—to watch their bond is indescribable. Nurses and doctors were shocked to walk in on their rounds and find a small baby who was content, happy, and quiet. Was this ideal? No. Hell, no, it wasn't ideal. A baby in one of the nastiest, germ-infested places, crawling around, playing with his toys? No. But what was ideal, though, was that we were together—every single hour of every single day. We played, slept, ate, laughed, cried, and snuggled together during every hospital stay. We were always there, fighting with Joe. The hospital staff knew they had three patients in our room, never just one. They cared for and took care of all of us, ensuring we had a room to ourselves, privacy when we needed it, and guidance as we planned to move forward. We fought cancer in 7D.

Many friends and family begged me to stay at their houses that were close to the hospital. I wasn't leaving though. I never left. My entire world was captured in our hospital room. I was uncomfortable and exhausted—mentally, emotionally, physically. I was depleted of energy and rarely slept, but we were together.

We often would be in the hospital for a week before the doctors would find the right combination of medication to control Joe's pain. It tore my heart out. I wanted to fix the cancer; I wanted to fix the pain. I couldn't seem to fix anything though.

Often, soon after returning home from these summer stays in the hospital, Joe would be immediately back into a level-ten pain again. He hated when the doctors asked him the question, "On a scale of 1 to 10, what is your pain?" I often was so sleep deprived, and beyond angry that we had gotten back to that point, that I spoke up and said any number beyond ten, explaining that he was in tears, screaming, and couldn't breathe due to the pain. Joe, somehow, tried to convince them it was never that bad. Maybe he had forgotten the nights I was up taking care of him, but I had not. I just wanted him to be comfortable.

Back and forth we went that summer. We would find a pain medication regimen that worked in the hospital, being administered intravenously, but then we would get home and find out the "equivalent" oral medication did not come close to touching the pain. Back to the hospital we went, with the secret bags packed, the phone call made for another pick-up and drop-off of belongings, and the argument to go back to the hospital.

Eventually, the doctors realized our home regimen was not working. They suggested we have an intrathecal pain pump, a hockey-puck-looking device, installed under the skin in Joe's lower right abdomen. The device connected to his spinal column, where it continually infused pain medication into his system. At allotted times, if the pain was still unmanageable, we could use a remote-control device that would give an extra push of medication into his system. This was in addition to many oral narcotics that he continued to take. Thankfully, Joe's pain was finally being managed effectively. His quality of life involved a lot of sleeping, with occasionally eating.

Not to be forgotten during our summer of pain was Joe's need to be outside in the warm weather. His body temperature never adjusted to the chemotherapy and his significant weight loss. He was always cold. Humidity in the Ozark Mountains during the summer is out-of-this-world. Our front porch proved to be the warmest place at home, and Joe often lay his frail body on a repurposed bench, dozing off in the warm air. Porter and I got to enjoy the warmth as we pulled all our toys to the front porch and played while Joe slept. The grim reality of our situation never seemed to deter us from spending time together. We were a young family, enjoying every milestone together. We never had work, or the busy lives that society tells us we need, interfere. Unlike our first wedding anniversary, which we celebrated together in the hospital, we celebrated our second wedding anniversary together in the warmth of our front porch. I had never been more grateful for any celebration than this day.

Chapter 23

Back to Work Round Two

With the summer winding down quickly, school would soon begin. In addition to our back-to-school teacher meetings near the middle of August, I needed to spend time in my classroom preparing for students to come. Fortunately, my school family rallied around us again. Our school librarian volunteered her time and resources to set up my classroom so I could cherish every last minute of that summer with Porter and Joe. Things were not going well, and everyone was aware of the downward spiral we were taking. We were anticipating another CT scan result. This time, the results would tell us if the chemotherapy was shrinking anything at all.

My second day of school was our son's first birthday, August 21, 2014. Requesting off for the day, I knew in my heart it was the last birthday we would get to celebrate together. The same day we celebrated Porter's year of blessings in our life, we went for our final scan and a day full of birthday shopping, just the three of us. The CT scan was carried out with specific instructions—not from the doctor, but from me. I demanded the results be held until after the weekend. Our son's first birthday party was that weekend, and we simply wanted to enjoy every moment without the unavoidable news lingering over us.

That evening, we celebrated Porter's birthday with presents of clothes, his first pair of Nike's, and a motorcycle Joe got to put together. Joe insisted upon sharing a slice of chocolate pie with Porter, one of Joe's happiest moments that entire year. Many things happened that day that, had Joe not been sick, would have frustrated me. I had perspective, though. Perspective reminded me that life's frustrations should not be exaggerated and that the little things should not be overlooked, but cherished. I knew what the CT scan was going to show, and that it wasn't good news. But I also knew that we got to celebrate a birthday that I thought we would never get to celebrate together.

That weekend we celebrated Porter's first birthday at our home with over eighty close friends and Joe's family. Parking was outrageous; the heat was blazing. In retrospect, I know those friends and family were there not just to celebrate Porter's first year of life. They were there to celebrate us. They were there because they saw what the disease was doing to Joe's body, and they wanted to honor us before it was too late. It was, indeed, the greatest celebration I have ever been a part of, a gathering no words can describe.

Chapter 24

The Call

Monday, August 25, 2014. I dreaded waking up that morning, knowing a phone call about Joe's CT scan was looming. I went about my day, dropping Porter off to daycare, teaching, and touching base with my principal, who knew I was expecting the phone call. I had met with her the week prior to explain our situation. An emotional conversation, I told her that things were spiraling fast, and I wanted no regrets. Sitting on her rectangular-seated stool, I confidently, and sadly, told her if things were progressing, I needed to stay home. I informed her I knew this school was still a business to run, and if they needed to let me go, I understood. And I did. My students still needed to learn, progress, and move forward. At this time, though, my husband was my number one priority. As tears streaked my face, my principal blessed me with her kindness: "I understand. We understand. We are all praying for you. Whatever we can do to help, we will." In that moment, she became much more than my boss. She became my friend.

The school day passed, and my phone was glued to my side. No call from the doctor's office. I picked up Porter from daycare and then went straight home to check on Joe. I hadn't heard much from him that day, but I knew he was still very tired from the birthday party two days earlier, so I wasn't too concerned. When we arrived home, we found Joe waiting for us on the front porch, perched on his usual bench, enjoying the warm temperatures outside. No words were exchanged about whether I had received the phone call. But I began to think I should call the doctor to confirm my suspicion about the CT scan results.

As dinnertime approached, Joe felt good enough to eat. The three of us sat at our island, overlooking the stillness of Table Rock Lake, our hearts quiet. Suddenly, my phone rang. I knew it was the doctor's office calling. My body stiffened from the shock of knowing what conversation I was about to have. My voice faltered as I cracked out, "Hello?" Our oncologist was on the other line with the results from the CT scan. I walked two steps away from the two people I love the most and escaped into our bedroom.

"Kristina, the results from the CT scan are here." A long pause ensued. "Kristina, I am sorry. The cancer is growing. The chemotherapy is not working."

Tears had already begun to spill onto my cheeks, even before I heard him say hello. I knew what he would tell me, but deep down, I was hoping he would prove me wrong. He did not.

Nodding my head up and down, as if the doctor could tell I understood, I frantically searched for words to respond. All the while, I demanded myself not to cry. I couldn't help it though. I already was. I heard Joe escape to the bathroom to lose what little he had just eaten. I let out a small gasp, knowing he couldn't hear me now.

"Okay," I sobbed. I managed to whisper, "What is the plan? What can we do?"

"We can attempt to put Joe on a chemotherapy pill. It is strong, something he will take daily. Let's plan on you guys coming in on Thursday for an appointment to discuss it."

I quickly agreed to meet on Thursday and hung up. I turned around, picked my son up out of his high chair, and put him down. As I began to walk back into our bedroom, Porter was right there with me. Our sweet, twelve-month-old, chunky-cheeked baby stood there, and I fell to my knees into his outstretched arms. That little baby's body molded into mine as he lay his sweet, precious head onto my shoulder. It was as if he knew the comfort his holding me brought. I sobbed. I sobbed and sobbed and sobbed into my infant's shoulder, begging God that this was not the end. The tears were immense, and I simply could not think of anything but a picture of what lay ahead—my own husband's funeral. I knew our fate, but I was still begging God to reverse it all.

I heard the toilet flush and the guest bathroom door open. I stifled every tear and ran into our master bathroom to try to conceal the remnant effects the phone call had on me. After a few swipes of makeup, and a mental conversation telling myself to pull it all together, I emerged. I told Joe the doctor called and had scheduled an appointment for us on Thursday. I could not tell him the whole truth of that conversation. I felt like a coward as I looked at my husband and uttered those words. My brain told me to tell the whole truth, but my mouth could not produce the syllables. My heart was too shattered to allow it to break any more by watching his reaction to the information I had just received.

After putting our son to bed, I drew scorching hot water into our bathtub. I rarely was able to do this, as our son was always wide awake unless my body heat touched his. Maybe God made an exception that night. I crawled into that bathtub and cried. When the tears became so intense that the pain would escape as moans and screams, I would lower myself underwater and cry until my lungs were about to explode. Eventually, I would emerge from the water, gasping for air and wondering what was next, and more importantly, when?

Chapter 25

The Plan

I went to work the next two days, knowing on Thursday I would not. I also knew that once we spoke with our oncologist, I probably would not be going to work for a while. Those two days lingered. Thursday morning finally came. The routine blood work and vitals went as expected. But as I anticipated the nearness of the conversation with the doctor, it felt like time slowed down. Sitting in the exam room and waiting for our oncologist were nothing new. But the tension, the high emotions, and the rawness of the inevitable were all there. I kept trying to ignore every one of the things I felt. I simply could not though. Joe was medicated enough that he seemed to be zoning out. He also didn't know the information I had kept from him, but even if he did, I think he would have attempted to keep it all together, for me anyways.

Our oncologist walked in and greeted Joe and me, as well as our sweet baby that he had watched grow since he was born. Darting his eye contact, I meekly gave my hello and looked down at anything in that white, sterile exam room except him. He went over vitals, which, in hindsight, I realize is nothing but small talk when you know what is about to be discussed. He stalled a little longer by entering his credentials into the computer to pull up the results.

Then, he said out loud what he had told me over the phone. The chemotherapy was not working. We could do an oral chemotherapy, a pill, which Joe would take every day. He went on to explain that this chemotherapy would have to come from a special pharmacy and that he would arrange for them to call me. The conversation went on without either Joe or I saying a word, only nodding our heads. I occasionally stole a look out of the corner of my eye to see Joe's reaction. Defeat. Severe depression. The onset of accepting what was going to happen. And I could not talk. The lump in my throat was far too large. Then, in awkward silence, Joe spoke up.

"What if it doesn't work? The oral chemo, what if it doesn't work?"

The tears flooded my face. That's what I wanted to know too, but I didn't have the guts to ask. Our oncologist looked down, I am certain checking his own emotion, and quietly responded with, "It will. It will."

Quickly, our doctor stood up and informed me I would receive a phone call within the next day to arrange for the oral chemotherapy to be delivered to us. He wished us the best of luck. After he exited, we sat there behind the closed door. I sat in that stiff, green hospital waiting chair, my dying husband next to me, our son in my lap. We sat, without words, without action. We sat in silence, both unable to look at each other, both unable to speak. Angry tears brimmed then fell past my eyelids. In this moment, like so many others, there were no words to say. I quickly grabbed his hand, pursed my lips together, and looked into his deep blue eyes—eyes that had tears falling from them, eyes that looked at me in desperation as if to say, "What are we going to do now?"

Since we both could not speak, we gathered our things to leave. We opened the exam room door that was directly across from the chemo room. Our nurses greeted us with hugs, smiles, and love—so did our co-warriors who we had shared this room with every other Thursday for the past year. The nurses looked quizzically at me, and from the tears I was fighting, they knew. Joe didn't say much either, but his affectionate hugs told our story. Our nurses knew, our regulars knew. Each person there that day attempted to keep their own emotions and tears in check. All that love, though, made it even harder to keep it together on our end. Only Porter, the one who always brought joy and smiles to the entire room, could distract everyone from the inevitable.

The ride home was silent. Given the circumstances, small talk was ridiculous—to this day, I hate it. My mind raced to try to find something to say, but each time I opened my mouth, I quickly closed it again. Anything I had thought to say seemed irrelevant. Once home, I called my principal to let her know our plan. I also let her know I wouldn't be at work the next day. I told her I might know what to do about work after I had a few days to process. Maybe the answer would come to me. Even that, though, proved wrong. No answers just came; there was no easy answer to any of this. I finally accepted that I would have to take it day-by-day. We didn't have a plan. How could you? We were just existing.

Chapter 26

Ungodly Pain

The days trucked on, and so did the intensity of Joe's pain. His pain was so immense that nothing could alleviate it. No one tells you about this pain—the body-encompassing, soul-grabbing pain that cancer gives you. Certainly, no one talks about how much the pain increases as the cancer grows. I knew that recovering from surgeries would be painful. Never did I know, however, the pain he would have because of the cancer itself. Watching Joe in such levels of pain was the most horrifying, mind-numbing experience I have ever had.

As Joe's pain increased, so did the amount of his medication. In addition to his intrathecal pain pump, which had already been adjusted to increase the dose of medication, Joe was getting his extra "pushes" of medication at the exact time it would allow for more. Honestly, we were usually a few minutes early, waiting for the pump to allow us to push more right at the minute it would allow for it. We also kept his oral narcotic medication going, which in and of itself, was more than Joe's weak, malnourished body should be able to handle. Even with all this pain medication, Joe was awake and alert—all the more proof that his pain really was that bad.

One night, Joe was screaming and rolling around in a ball on our bedroom floor. Crying with him, I attempted to calm him by leading him through deep breathing exercises. I tried to lay him on his back, lifting his legs up on the wall, to relieve some pressure off his back. I offered to rub his back, but he refused, not wanting anything or anyone to touch him. Nothing was touching the pain. This pain was different than any of the other pain that had made an appearance during his illness. We checked into the hospital, hoping for some relief.

We had been back to the hospital multiple times that fall. Each time, our nurses, who knew our situation, were ready and worked quickly to get the IV of drugs into Joe's system, which provided some relief. This night, though, there was no relief. The on-call oncologists were horrified, and I am certain annoyed, that our nurses continued to call them to tell them nothing was working. At one point, a night nurse told us the on-call doctor told them not to call again until a certain amount of time had passed.

Furious, sleep deprived, and climbing the walls trying to find Joe any relief, I began screaming. Joe, propped up in his hospital bed, could not stop moving. His legs moved up and down, over and over. He moved to the floor. He moved back to the bed, only reversed so his legs were propped up with his head at the foot of the bed. He turned, he rolled, he crawled into a ball. He continued to cry over and over. He asked me in between gasps of air, "Why? Why me? Why is this happening, Baby?" I was bawling. For the first time in our over-a-year-long battle, we allowed ourselves to cry in front of each other that night. I could never pray with Joe—not out loud. I would have cried, and he would have too. We had prayed silently up until that night. And upon his "Whys?" to me, upon his begging for relief, I sat on the floor, touching him, and I cried out myself:

"God, please. Please, I am begging you. Do anything, anything God. I cannot watch him suffer like this anymore. I am begging you, God, take him if you must take him. Please just do not make him suffer anymore."

Joe chimed in during this cry out to God, and he himself begged God for the same. Between cries, screams of pain, moaning, sobbing and defeat, some nurse had mercy on us and called the on-call doctor even though it was not yet time. The pain medication was upped to a level I am certain the doctor was not comfortable with, and Joe finally got some rest that night. I, however, watched him sleep. I watched his chest rise and fall, over and over and over that night. I watched him at peace for the first time in days. I gently kissed Joe's hand, his forehead, his cheek, and then did the same to our sweet baby lying in my arms.

The next morning the phantom on-call doctor approached our room. Upon entering, the shock on his face that Joe was awake and alert enough to speak with him was evident. Given the levels of medication they had administered overnight, he was in awe that Joe was not still sedated. He explained his hesitation in upping our pain medication because it was already at a dangerous level given Joe's weight and situation.

Our oncologist, aware of the what had transpired the night before, made his rounds later that morning. He did his usual— listened to Joe's lungs, looked into his eyes, and examined his body. I requested to step out of the room with him. As I walked into the hallway, Joe nodded off to sleep. Quietly shutting the door behind me, while gently bouncing Porter up and down in my arms, I asked our oncologist, point blank, "How long? How long do we have?" Our doctor always seemed squeamish when I would ask this, or anything remotely close to this question.

He looked down and responded, "Are you off work now?"

"Yes, that's why I am here with him. Every time I am here with him."

"Good," he responded, "You should be home with him." His eyes darted away from mine as he looked down the empty hallway.

What did that mean anyways? Choked up, and that lump cutting off my air supply, I could barely choke out, "But how long do you think?"

"There really is no known time."

Throughout our entire journey, I found myself angry that I continued to get this answer. No one–not our regular oncologist, not our surgeon, not even our doctors we received a second opinion from in St. Louis—would give me a timeline or even an estimate of how much time we had. In hindsight, I realize that they probably didn't want to be wrong. You hear stories every day of doctors guessing this number incorrectly. I rationalized my need to know for work—although it didn't really matter. I was going to stay home with him as much as I could. My school and community knew our situation and supported every decision we made. I like to plan though. And there was no planning this out. I was scared to death I wouldn't be home when "it" happened. I was scared to death I would wake up one morning, home by myself with our baby, when "it" happened. There was no timeframe given. After all—there is only One who knew the real answer to this. He made sure my fears of missing "it" were unfounded.

Chapter 27

Final Days

After too many hospital stays to address Joe's pain, I took an indefinite leave of absence from school. I informed the parents of my students, all of whom were completely supportive, of my decision. I still worried about my classroom but also had to let my type-A personality take a break as my priorities shifted. Joe's health was declining, and I knew these moments at home would be the last cherished moments we would have as a family. Teachers stepped up, long-term substitutes were found, and my paraprofessional ensured my class never missed a beat.

Our days were simple. We rarely left the house, except to report to the doctor's office for lab work and routine vitals. Joe moved frequently between the bed and the recliner in our bedroom, always wrapped in an electric blanket with the TV remote in hand. The television was a temporary escape from our reality. Joe's favorite shows about traveling, antiques, and car restorations drew his interest enough to stay awake, sometimes anyways. Most of the time, though, Joe slept.

Within our final three weeks, Joe awoke from a nap and joined Porter and me in the kitchen for an early afternoon lunch. As I fed the baby and chatted about work, Porter's silly personality, and how close he was to walking, Joe said something startling. He chuckled and said, "Those people are funny."

I froze, looked up at him, and asked, "What did you say?"

Munching on a chip, he chuckled again and said, "Those people over there. They are funny." He nodded his head in the direction of our kitchen windows. I turned to look behind me, to find no one there at all. Alarmed, frightened, and flabbergasted, I slowly corrected him, "Baby, there are no people over there."

"Yes, there are. Right there, Babe. Aren't they funny?"

I knew in this moment things were not right. I never considered that this was just his medication talking—he had been on extremely high dosages for a very long time. We had never experienced anything like this. I smiled back at him and knew. I knew then that God was not going to reverse this. I knew for sure our fate and that it was going to take place soon. I quickly called our doctor and requested that he ask hospice to contact me.

At that point, I didn't really understand what hospice is, other than what I had heard from various sources. I only knew that I needed help knowing what was normal, and what was not normal. I didn't tell Joe that hospice was coming for a visit, only that there would be someone coming to the house to discuss doing his vitals at home weekly, rather than going to the doctor's office. I'm not sure why I was worried that Joe would find out. In between all his sleeping, he didn't really notice who was at our house, or why they were there.

During our first intake meeting, our nurse did the normal vitals and asked questions about Joe's pain and medications he was taking, including his oral chemotherapy pills. She also asked questions about my needs: picking up medications, someone sitting with Joe while I ran errands, help with our son. I turned down help for all those things. I knew I could still handle those, but I knew I needed someone I could call who would be here if anything strange or abnormal happened. She agreed and said she would make once-a-week visits, unless we needed her more.

Strange things continued to happen. Joe slept most of every day. The few scarce minutes he didn't sleep, though, were always out-of-the-normal experiences. He called a decorative fall display on our mantle a watermelon instead of a pumpkin. When I didn't know what he was talking about, he became emotional and told me to stop making him feel "stupid." These reactions were so out of character, and seeing him so upset and insulted crushed me too. We both cried, me sitting on the floor in between his legs, him holding my head and rubbing my hair.

A couple of weeks after hospice's initial visit, our school and community rallied behind us and set up a Color Run fundraiser at our town's annual fall festival. All proceeds went to our family to help us pay expenses and bills. This was especially helpful due to my being off work so long. Not one day passed in the weeks leading up to the event that Joe didn't talk about the 5K Color Run approaching and look forward to being there.

The day of the 5K Color Run was a gloomy and rainy Saturday. Joe's family and our school family—those who fought every day with us—were there to support us. Girls from my basketball team showed up in matching blue tutus and handmade shirts to show their support for us. My school district's administrators, teachers, students, and even staff members I didn't know were there to support us. Even some of Joe's friends from high school, who he had not seen in years, showed up to support us. We were truly loved that day. Joe did not talk crazy, he was not sick, and he was not in any pain. I knew it was our final celebration.

Not long after the Color Run, Joe's best friend from high school, Travis, stopped by our house for his typical weekly visit. His visits always proved to brighten Joe's spirits, and mine too. We always looked forward to his visits. He usually brought us a cooked meal or two and did anything I needed him to do. This particular week, we needed to take Joe to the doctor's office for his weekly vital check-up instead of hospice coming to our house.

Travis requested to take Joe to his appointment so I could run to my basketball team's season-opening meeting at the school. After a quick two hours, I was home, but Travis and Joe were not. I frantically texted and called Travis to ensure all was okay. It was. Travis told me that they had done some shopping and that Joe had found a scrap piece of granite for our mantle. They would be home soon. Unbeknownst to me, he had also found something else while he was in town.

Once they arrived home, Travis began pacing around our house, as nervous as I had ever seen him. Stumbling and stuttering over his words, he eventually begged me for forgiveness for the item Joe had purchased while they were in town. Confused, I asked what he meant. Travis told me that Joe persuaded him to stop at a pawn shop. Why? To this day, I am not certain. We had never stopped at the pawn shop before. But he did that day. Once there, he purchased a hunting rifle. Just like that. Joe had never even mentioned he wanted a hunting rifle. Joe rarely, if ever, hunted. He bought a gun though. Travis told me he tried to talk Joe out of it and asked him if he thought I would like this idea. Joe, heavily sedated and losing touch with reality, insisted it was fine.

I don't know that it was fine, but at that moment, I wasn't sure what else to say. I, of course, immediately asked Joe about this purchase. Much like a little boy, he smiled broadly and told me he got what he had always wanted. Though I was not sure I understood, since he had never expressed this desire to me, I smiled back at the innocence in his eyes and his face. He was beginning to tire already, and as his body began to relax into the couch, I could tell sleep was about to take him under.

I asked, "Honey, what money did you use to buy this gun?" I was concerned. Since I managed the finances and paid the bills since he got sick, I knew we had $93 in our checking account. I also knew my pay check would continue to be docked due to not being at work. Shockingly, Joe whispered, "The money I had in my wallet. Don't worry, Babe, we have plenty of money in the bank."

"No, Babe, we have $93 in our checking account."

"Ninety-three hundred dollars is plenty. The gun wasn't that expensive."

"BABE, I said $93, as in less than $100. We don't even have $100 in our account."

As his head leaned back and his eyes closed, Joe smiled, completely at ease and without worry, and drifted off to sleep.

Joe had not been anywhere without me, except that day with Travis. There was nowhere he could have gotten money without my knowing, was there? Later that day, I asked to see his wallet. There I found a very large amount of money and asked him where he got it. He responded with, "Friends. Friends at the race."

I never knew. I still do not know who those people were who gave him all that money. I just know that the money given to us and donated on our behalf during our cancer journey saved our family from losing our home, from worrying about how to pay bills, and it allowed our family to spend every moment together during those last weeks, rather than worrying about work. This is just one example of the very worst situations bringing out the very best in this world.

Chapter 28

The Last 48 Hours

Joe's need to sleep increased even more. When he was awake, he would graze in the pantry and talk with Porter and me. Only, most things he said didn't make sense at all. Attempting to hide my broken heart, I would smile and nod along to whatever he had said. Heartache consumed me. I knew what was happening, but I was still praying for God to show up and reverse what seemed to be inevitable.

On Friday, October 24, 2014, our baby was asleep in the middle of our king-sized bed. Joe had been up for a few minutes to get his pain medication, and then he said, "In bed with me, in bed with me, get in bed. Next to me, next to me, right next to me." He said this over and over as I attempted to swallow the tears, thinking this was it. I helped him into our bed, gently scooped our baby up and moved him to the side of the bed and wedged myself right in between them. Like our small baby to the right of me, my sweet husband crawled into a ball up against my body and asked me to hold him. The way his voice sounded so distant, so far away, so not there with me caused heartbreak I cannot put into words. I complied with his rambling requests and held him in my arms.

His smile was genuine, comfortable, and he fell asleep. I did not. I lay there, watching him, crying softly, beginning to accept what was inevitable, knowing this one of the last times his body and mine would mold together in our bed. I knew it was one of the last moments I would feel his beating heart next to my chest, and that our hearts would soon stop beating to the same beat. I knew this was one of our last moments, the three of us who love each other without measure, snuggled up together as one unit. I knew.

Knowing how much time we had left is what I wanted to know our whole journey. I changed my mind that night. I didn't want to know now. I didn't want to be alone when Joe's time was near. I still cannot explain it, but lying there sobbing that night, I sent out a text to his aunts, uncles, and cousins and called his parents. I told them I thought it was close and I needed them to come. Despite many living more than three hours away, they all were present first thing the next morning. I also asked his closest friends to come if they wanted to say good-bye.

We began to have more and more visitors; each one Joe acknowledged with a slight opening of his eyes before he nodded back off. Each one, in reply, began to choke back tears or allowed their emotions to show and sobbed. After about an hour, Joe did not wake up anymore. I remember shaking him a little harder, longer, attempting to tell him his life-long friend was here to say hi. But he did not open his eyes. With our son watching, I attempted to control my panic. My mind raced; my heart caught. At the same time I was trying to control my every emotion, I was also trying to control what was happening to Joe. I couldn't though. I shook harder, longer. Still nothing. The realization grasped my throat, my breathing stopped, and I looked at everyone in our bedroom who blankly stared back at me. They knew the end was near and it was inevitable. They were waiting for my reaction.

I lay next to Joe in his recliner. And for the first time, right in front of my dying husband, I screamed, cried, and let out every ounce of pain I had bottled inside for the past sixteen months. At some point, everyone excused themselves and took our baby with them, leaving the two of us alone. I begged him not to go, not to leave us, not to do this to me. I reminded him I needed him to do life with, to raise our child with, to be loved. I apologized for anything I ever did or said that disappointed him or hurt him. I told him I would change places with him right this minute, that Porter needed him more than he needed me. I begged him to forgive me for not finding a cure, for not finding an answer to all of this. I asked him to watch over our baby all the times I could not. I pleaded with him to send reminders through our son when I needed to know he was still close. And over and over and over again, I prayed to God to please not let this happen. I'd trade everything He had ever given me if He would spare my husband. I needed him to spare my husband for me, for Porter, for our family. I would do anything else, lose anything else, but not my husband.

And then when I could not utter another audible word, I sobbed. I lay at my husband's feet, in the fetal position, and I sobbed every ounce of energy out of my body. Joe's Aunt Carolyn eventually came in to calm me, soothe me, cry with me. Joe, still peacefully sitting in his recliner, appeared to not have heard a word I said. I knew he did though. In the deepest part of my heart, I knew he did.

Each of Joe's family and friends took time to say good-byes, to cry, and to say what needed to be said. Later that day, Joe frightened me when he grabbed himself, indicating he needed to use the restroom. I had assumed he would not interact with us anymore. I was wrong. Since his legs did not work, I did my best, with the help of his dad and uncle, to get him to the restroom. My modest husband was not about to allow the end of his life to be the time he had an accident. Neither was I. I wanted him to have everything he needed to go in peace.

Family members dispersed around our home to sleep, knowing each minute was closer to the inevitable. Sunday, October 26, 2014, every minute was a fight. Joe was so much different this day than the day prior. He didn't sleep but was alert all day. He wanted back in bed. He was interacting, if that is what you could call it. Nothing he tried to say made any sense. It was all gibberish, but he said it adamantly, with confidence. He was trying to tell us something and only grew more frustrated when only sounds would come out. I lay right there with him, crying, asking, trying to figure out what he was saying. Joe threw the covers off and pulled them back on. He attempted to get out of bed and pushed away help, resulting in a fall. Joe's frustration grew; it was clear he wanted something but could not communicate it. He sat up, legs over the side of the bed, muttered sounds, grew angry, and then lay down again.

Eventually, Joe's frustration grew to an all-time high. I figured out from his sounds and pointing that he wanted his chair. I moved the chair closer to our bed so he could sit in it. More sounds and muttering, hands holding his head in anger, more tears streaming down my face trying to figure out what he was saying. His mind made up, he managed to articulate, "My boy." Voice quivering, gasping for air, I managed, "You want Porter?" Another nod of his head yes, and someone brought Porter to us.

There we were. Joe, Porter, his parents, and I crouched around him, crying, attempting to figure out what he was trying to tell us. And there, in that moment, Joe offered a passionate speech. The words were not audible. They were sounds, so mangled together that no one could understand anything he was saying. He was so passionate though—words spewing, voice rising and falling. He wanted us to know. And we all sat there, sobbing, nodding our heads yes, acknowledging that we were right there with him, for him.

Not much later, Joe indicated he needed to go to the restroom again. His arms draped over me and his dad's shoulders, he tried to pull us into the direction of our guest bathroom for privacy. Angry, letting out a moan, I cried more and tried to explain he was not strong enough to go in there. I sat him down on the toilet in our bathroom and stayed there to hold him up because he could not sit upright on his own. His modesty still in check, he pushed me away. I sobbed uncontrollably, trying to persuade him I had to be in there with him so he did not fall. When he was finished, I cleaned him up. He never wanted me to have to do this. He responded with a scream of disgrace, and I knew that with this act I had taken his dignity from him.

His dad and I got him back to our bed, a short five steps away. Continually restless, he said his only other audible word that day. After a full sixty seconds of fighting to get the word out, he shouted, "BATH!" I asked him if he wanted a bath. He nodded his head yes, and I looked up in desperation at his dad and uncle.

My mind raced to figure out how to grant him this wish. I asked a family member to grab a bag-chair off our front porch. We set the chair in the shower, and Joe's dad and uncle helped Joe back to our bathroom. Carefully, I undressed my dying husband, slowly moving his body like an infant who had no control over his body parts. I sat him in the shower and climbed in fully clothed. There, I washed my husband's body for the very last time. I stood in our shower, Joe's dad and uncle watching me sob uncontrollably as I washed my husband's hair, his near-lifeless body sitting in the chair, the warm water hitting his body. Shutting the water off, I placed a towel around him, while his dad and uncle held him up. After we dressed him in fresh clothing, we carefully walked him back to our bed. His final wish was fulfilled.

After changing into dry clothing, I crawled up next to him, and laid my head on his shoulder.

Sobbing, choking, I managed: "You can go, Baby. I'll be okay. I don't want you to suffer anymore. I hate watching you in pain."

Somehow, Joe wrapped his right arm around me and looked straight at me. He then pushed me away.

Barely audible, I confessed, "I lied. I never want you to go, Joe. Never. I don't know how I will live without you. But please, I don't want you to suffer anymore. I will suffer the rest of my life missing you so you don't have to suffer anymore."

Within five minutes, Joe took a large gasp of air, and I watched his chest rise differently. His eyes were set towards the ceiling, and our hospice nurse confirmed what I already knew. Her stethoscope on his chest, she looked at me and shook her head. And I ended our fight with cancer the same exact way we started it, "NOOOOOOOOOOOOOOOOOO!!!!!!!!!!!!" Both of our hearts stopped beating that day.

Epilogue

Planning a funeral for my husband at age twenty-five was not what I envisioned for my life. The finality of that day was a hard pill to swallow, but I was resolved to keep the many promises I had made to Joe through our fight of colon cancer.

Five months before he passed, we discussed my pursuing a Master's Degree in Education Administration. My husband encouraged me, then made me promise I would finish it. Only two months prior to his passing, in the midst of all we had going on, I began my classes. I am certain he knew the wisdom in that promise. He knew I would need something to hold onto, to work towards, to preoccupy my thoughts, to distract me from my sadness and grieving heart. I pursued and graduated with my Master of Education Administration from Lindenwood University in St. Louis, Missouri, in May 2016.

Joe told me many times through our battle I would write a book one day. Shocked, I asked, "About what?"

He replied, "This. Us. Our journey." Thinking he was crazy, I nodded my head and agreed with him so we could leave the subject. Again, he knew what would be best for me. Writing this book has allowed me to process, to heal, and to experience his love all over again. It has proven even more beneficial for my heart than I could have ever imagined. He was right—I would write a book.

In the final forty-eight hours with Joe, although he did not talk back to me, I could oddly feel his responses. The moment we all gathered around him as he passionately tried to tell us something, I knew in my heart he was telling me to take good care of our son and to raise him into a man. Until the day I meet my husband again in Heaven, I promised my husband and best friend I would do the best I could to raise our son into the man Joe was.

In addition, unexpected healing has taken place as I have become an Ambassador and Advocate for Fight CRC, a nonprofit organization for research, detection, and awareness for colorectal cancer. Participating in a nationwide PSA, guest blogging, attending Call-On-Congress 2017 and 2018 in Washington D.C. to speak to our senators and representatives, and connecting with others who have been affected by the second-most deadly cancer in the United States has given me purpose in grief. We are not alone in this fight, and we must find a cure. More information can be found at FightCRC.org.

After attending the 2017 Call on Congress, another national not-for-profit organization, The Colon Club, reached out to me for their advocacy efforts with colon cancer affecting those under the age of fifty. The Colon Club publishes an annual magazine, "On the Rise," featuring colon cancer survivors, fighters, and for the first time, caregivers, that were affected by this disease before the age of fifty. As one of the first caregivers to be featured in this magazine, I am honored to carry on the fight for my "colon brothers and sisters."

I also got to attend a week-long summer retreat with others who understand the colon cancer journey and each heart-wrenching milestone; this proved to be a week of healing. I was recently appointed Vice President of Communications and Operations for The Colon Club. The organization only utilizes volunteers, and I joyfully serve in this position as a way to give back to those affected by colon cancer. More information can be found at ColonClub.com.

Our son continues to thrive, as his dad would want him to. He is a spitting image of his daddy on the inside and out. Since Joe has been gone, I have witnessed many miracles. He sends messages and signs through Porter, as he promised, to let me know he is close. Porter does things exactly like Joe did. And, I have witnessed our son having a conversation with his dad. Porter often tells me of dreams he has about his dad and of things his dad has come to tell him. He tells me things that he could never have known about his dad unless, of course, his dad really told him these things.

For all these reasons and more, I know miracles are real. We prayed for a miracle. We didn't get what we expected. We got so many more.

Made in the USA
Middletown, DE
27 April 2019